ESP8266 Home Automation Projects

Leverage the power of this tiny WiFi chip to build exciting smart home projects

Catalin Batrinu

BIRMINGHAM - MUMBAI

ESP8266 Home Automation Projects

First published: November 2017

Production reference: 2091118

Published by Packt Publishing Ltd.
Livery Place
35 Livery Street
Birmingham
B3 2PB, UK.
ISBN 978-1-78728-262-9

www.packtpub.com

Credits

Author
Catalin Batrinu

Reviewer
Constantin Tambrea

Acquisition Editor
Prachi Bisht

Content Development Editor
Eisha Dsouza

Technical Editor
Naveenkumar Jain

Copy Editor
Safis Editing

Project Coordinator
Kinjal Bari

Proofreader
Safis Editing

Indexer
Francy Puthiry

Graphics
Tania Dutta

Production Coordinator
Melwyn Dsa

About the Author

Catalin Batrinu graduated from the Politehnica University of Bucharest in Electronics, Telecommunications, and Information Technology. He has been working as a software developer in telecommunications for the past 16 years. He has worked with old protocols and the latest network protocols and technologies, so he has experienced all the recent transformations in the telecommunications industry. He has implemented many telecommunications protocols, from access adaptations and backbone switches to high-capacity, carrier-grade switches on various hardware platforms from Wintegra and Broadcom.

The Internet of Things came as a natural evolution for him and now he collaborates with different companies to construct the world of tomorrow, which will make our life more comfortable and secure. Using the ESP8266, he has prototyped devices such as irrigation controllers, smart sockets, window shutters, digital addressable lighting controls, and environment controls, all of them controlled directly from a mobile application via the cloud. An MQTT broker with bridging and a WebSockets server was even developed for the ESP8266. Soon, these devices will be part of our daily lives, so we will all enjoy their functionality.

Don't forget to then keep an eye on his blog `https://myesp8266.blogspot.com` and on the new platform as a service that you will discover soon at `https://iotcentral.eu`.

About the Reviewer

Constantin Tambrea has been a senior software engineer at Luxoft Romania for more than 9 years, and has been involved in various projects in the telecommunications field. He holds master's and bachelor's degrees in Computer Science from University Politehnica in Bucharest. His main domains of interest are Java Enterprise applications and web development techniques, but recently he has become passionate about the Internet of Things domain, in which he is experimenting with a personal home automation project.

I would like to give thanks to Catalin Batrinu, my colleague, and friend, for introducing me to the IoT world and for encouraging me to review his work on this book.

www.PacktPub.com

For support files and downloads related to your book, please visit www.PacktPub.com.

Did you know that Packt offers eBook versions of every book published, with PDF and ePub files available? You can upgrade to the eBook version at www.PacktPub.comand as a print book customer, you are entitled to a discount on the eBook copy. Get in touch with us at service@packtpub.com for more details.

At www.PacktPub.com, you can also read a collection of free technical articles, sign up for a range of free newsletters and receive exclusive discounts and offers on Packt books and eBooks.

https://www.packtpub.com/mapt

Get the most in-demand software skills with Mapt. Mapt gives you full access to all Packt books and video courses, as well as industry-leading tools to help you plan your personal development and advance your career.

Why subscribe?

- Fully searchable across every book published by Packt
- Copy and paste, print, and bookmark content
- On demand and accessible via a web browser

Customer Feedback

Thanks for purchasing this Packt book. At Packt, quality is at the heart of our editorial process. To help us improve, please leave us an honest review on this book's Amazon page at https://www.amazon.com/dp/1787282627. If you'd like to join our team of regular reviewers, you can email us at customerreviews@packtpub.com. We award our regular reviewers with free eBooks and videos in exchange for their valuable feedback. Help us be relentless in improving our products!

Table of Contents

Preface

Since the first house was built, man has made a conscious effort to improve it, to make it more comfortable and safe. Home automation or domotics has been around since decades in terms of lighting and simple appliance control and only recently has technology caught up for the idea of the interconnected world, allowing full control of your home from anywhere, to become a reality.

ESP8266 is a low-priced chip that allows you to build home automation system effectively. This book will demonstrate a few easy-to-implement home automation projects ranging from controlling a relay, to reading all kinds of parameters such as temperature, humidity, light, or presence. It also allows you to send the values from your ESP8266 modules to your private cloud. More than that, you will design and build a secure cloud and a mobile application that can bring comfort and safety at your fingertips. By the end of this book, you will be capable of building your own interconnected devices for better living.

There are many choices available in the market and you can choose your own ESP8266 module based on your project needs. Some of the widely accepted home automation projects are building a portable environmental monitor, wireless remote LCD, Air Gesture AC Dimmer/Switch, Wi-Fi Smart Garage Door, IoT Air Freshener, and internet-enabled smoke alarm.

Home automation is definitely here to stay as it continues to fill the needs of consumers who are looking for better ways to access information and control the home environment. With home automation, you can control your device the way you want.

What this book covers

Chapter 1, *Getting Started with the ESP8266*, covers the basics of the ESP8266 Wi-Fi chip, including how to choose a module, and how to configure the ESP8266 chip. You will learn how to configure the ESP8266 board, so it can be used for the rest of the book. You will know how to choose the right ESP8266 module as there are many choices available on the market. After that, you will learn the basics of the ESP8266 Wi-Fi chip, and learn how to read data from a sensor connected to the chip.

Chapter 2, *Building and Configuring Your Own MQTT Server*, speaks about building and configuring an MQTT server to be used with the ESP8266. The chapter will instruct you on how to get, compile, install, and configure an MQTT server to be used in the chapters as a central MQTT gateway.

Chapter 3, *Building a Home Thermostat with the ESP8266*, covers how to build a home thermostat using the ESP8266. You will learn how to measure the temperature in your home using a thermostat, how to display this temperature on a screen, and also how to adjust the temperature according to your wishes.

Chapter 4, *Control Appliances from the ESP8266*, shows how to control home appliances that are often present in a house, such as lamps, LEDs, and other appliances. You will learn how to control several home appliances using only the ESP8266 Wi-Fi chip. Thanks to the Wi-Fi connectivity of the chip, you will be able to control all the appliances remotely.

Chapter 5, *Using ESP8266 to Build a Security System*, covers how to build a complete security system based on the ESP8266. You will learn how to connect to your ESP8266 module's elements that are necessary to a security system, such as motion detectors, cameras, and alarms. You will then be able to build a complete security system based on these elements.

Chapter 6, *Securing Your Data*, This chapter is about adding SSL to secure communication between the ESP8266 modules and broker. You will learn to encrypt the packets in order to secure the data and make sure that your communication remains private.

Chapter 7, *Real-Time communication*, there are some use cases where you need to see data retrieved from the sensors in real time, to log the values in a database or to show them on a nice graph.

Chapter 8, *Adding a Mobile Application to Your Smart Home*, to complete the journey in the smart home world and have your house in control from your phone, you will create an Android mobile application.

What you need for this book

In order to start working with ESP8266, you will need a series of software and hardware components.
The ESP8266 chip and its module, sensors like ADXL345, temperature sensors, PIR sensors, and cables, soldering tools. In every chapter, I've tried to make a good picture and provide the good description.

For the software, we would require PC with Windows and VirtualBox installed. For application Arduino IDE with at least 1.5.3 SDK version for the ESP8266, Lubuntu Linux 16.04 installed in Virtual Box, Docker installed in Virtual Box, InfluxDB and Grafana installed in Virtual Box.

Who this book is for

This book is for people who want to build connections and inexpensive home automation projects using the ESP8266 Wi-Fi chip, and to completely automate their homes. A basic understanding of the board would be an added advantage.

Conventions

In this book, you will find a number of text styles that distinguish between different kinds of information. Here are some examples of these styles and an explanation of their meaning.

Code words in text, database table names, folder names, filenames, file extensions, pathnames, dummy URLs, user input, and Twitter handles are shown as follows: "The following is the setup() function to connect to the Wi-Fi network."

A block of code is set as follows:

```
#include <ESP8266WiFi.h>
#include <JsonListener.h>
#include "WundergroundClient.h"
```

Any command-line input or output is written as follows:

```
sudo openssl rsa -in ca.crt -out newca.pem
```

New terms and **important words** are shown in bold. Words that you see on the screen, for example, in menus or dialog boxes, appear in the text like this: "Click on **Sign in to network**."

Warnings or important notes appear in a box like this.

Tips and tricks appear like this.

Reader feedback

Feedback from our readers is always welcome. Let us know what you think about this book-what you liked or disliked. Reader feedback is important for us as it helps us develop titles that you will really get the most out of.

To send us general feedback, simply e-mail `feedback@packtpub.com`, and mention the book's title in the subject of your message.

If there is a topic that you have expertise in and you are interested in either writing or contributing to a book, see our author guide at `www.packtpub.com/authors`.

Customer support

Now that you are the proud owner of a Packt book, we have a number of things to help you to get the most from your purchase.

Downloading the example code

You can download the example code files for this book from your account at `http://www.packtpub.com`. If you purchased this book elsewhere, you can visit `http://www.packtpub.com/support` and register to have the files e-mailed directly to you.

You can download the code files by following these steps:

1. Log in or register to our website using your e-mail address and password.
2. Hover the mouse pointer on the **SUPPORT** tab at the top.
3. Click on **Code Downloads & Errata**.
4. Enter the name of the book in the **Search** box.
5. Select the book for which you're looking to download the code files.
6. Choose from the drop-down menu where you purchased this book from.
7. Click on **Code Download**.

Once the file is downloaded, please make sure that you unzip or extract the folder using the latest version of:

- WinRAR / 7-Zip for Windows
- Zipeg / iZip / UnRarX for Mac
- 7-Zip / PeaZip for Linux

The code bundle for the book is also hosted on GitHub at `https://github.com/ PacktPublishing/ESP8226_Home_Automation_Projects`. We also have other code bundles from our rich catalog of books and videos available at `https://github.com/ PacktPublishing/`. Check them out!

Downloading the color images of this book

We also provide you with a PDF file that has color images of the screenshots/diagrams used in this book. The color images will help you better understand the changes in the output. You can download this file from `http://www.packtpub.com/sites/default/files/ downloads/ESP8226HomeAutomationProjects_ColorImages.pdf`.

Errata

Although we have taken every care to ensure the accuracy of our content, mistakes do happen. If you find a mistake in one of our books-maybe a mistake in the text or the code- we would be grateful if you could report this to us. By doing so, you can save other readers from frustration and help us improve subsequent versions of this book. If you find any errata, please report them by visiting `http://www.packtpub.com/submit-errata`, selecting your book, clicking on the **Errata Submission Form** link, and entering the details of your errata. Once your errata are verified, your submission will be accepted and the errata will be uploaded to our website or added to any list of existing errata under the Errata section of that title.

To view the previously submitted errata, go to `https://www.packtpub.com/books/ content/support` and enter the name of the book in the search field. The required information will appear under the **Errata** section.

Piracy

Piracy of copyrighted material on the Internet is an ongoing problem across all media. At Packt, we take the protection of our copyright and licenses very seriously. If you come across any illegal copies of our works in any form on the Internet, please provide us with the location address or website name immediately so that we can pursue a remedy.

Please contact us at `copyright@packtpub.com` with a link to the suspected pirated material.

We appreciate your help in protecting our authors and our ability to bring you valuable content.

Questions

If you have a problem with any aspect of this book, you can contact us at questions@packtpub.com, and we will do our best to address the problem.

Getting Started with the ESP8266

1

It is impossible not to hear about the **Internet of Things (IoT)**, which is starting to enter into our homes and our lives, together with the necessity of consuming and controlling a huge amount of data every day. We all carry an internet-connected smartphone and we are able to instantly find and connect with people around the world.

If we are able to connect and discuss with people around the world, why not control our houses, our cars, and our offices from our smartphone? This is where the IoT comes into the picture and lets us connect almost any object to the internet.

Currently, there are a few chips that are capable of internet connection in the market but one little fellow has attracted developers' attention because of its features and price.

This chip is ESP8266, a low-cost TCP/IP and a Wi-Fi enabled microcontroller developed by EspressIf Systems, a company located in Shanghai, and we will find out more about it in this book. In this chapter, we will cover the following topics:

- Installing Arduino IDE
- Configuring the Arduino IDE for ESP8266
- Discovering ESP8266
- Connecting your ESP to a Wi-Fi network

Starting with the ESP8266 chip

In order to start working with ESP8266, you will need a series of software and hardware components. ESP8266 is a 32-bit RISC low-cost microcontroller with Wi-Fi connectivity, capable of running at 80 MHz or 160 MHz. It has 64 KiB of instruction RAM and 96 KiB of RAM data.

For firmware and other data storage, an external QSPI flash is connected to it and the size can vary from 512 KiB to 4 MiB. The chip itself exposes 16 **General Purpose Input/Output (GPIO)** pins but some of them are used for the QSPI flash connection. The remaining pins are capable of **Serial Peripheral Interface (SPI)**, I^2C, I^2S, **Universal Asynchronous Receiver/Transmitter (UART)**, and one 10-bit **Analog to Digital Converter (ADC)**.

The Wi-Fi capabilities are according to IEEE 80.11 b/g/n and provide WPA/WPA2 and WEP authentication but can also connect to open networks.

For this chapter, you will need just an ESP8266 module of your choice, since nowadays, there are many producers and board types available.

A good board can be found on `Sparkfun.com` or on e-commerce sites, such as `banggood.com`, or `aliexpress.com` but don't stop searching for them at your local electronics stores.

Now, the form factor of your board depends on your project constraints but for getting started with this chip, we can use one of the following boards:

- Witty ESP12-F board
- NodeMCU v1.0
- WeeMos D1 mini

Either board will work fine but if you are a beginner, I'd recommend you to start with the Witty ESP12-F board because it already has:

- **LDR (Light Dependent Resistor)** connected to the analog A0 input
- RGB LED connected to GPIO 15, GPIO 12, and GPIO13
- A push button connected to GPIO 4

Later, when we add other sensors to ESP8266, this module can be replaced with any of the other ESP8266 modules.

Installing Arduino IDE

ESP8266 can be used with the official EspressIf's SDKs that contain the NonOS and FreeRTOS SDKs writing code in C/C++, but other companies and people add other programming languages to it, such as Lua, Javascript, or MicroPhyton.

This book will use the NonOS SDK and as a development IDE, the Arduino IDE. In this part you will download the Arduino Software (IDE), configure it and install the ESP8266 SDK.

Downloading the Arduino Software IDE

To download the Arduino IDE, go to `https://www.arduino.cc/en/Main/Software` and download the latest version:

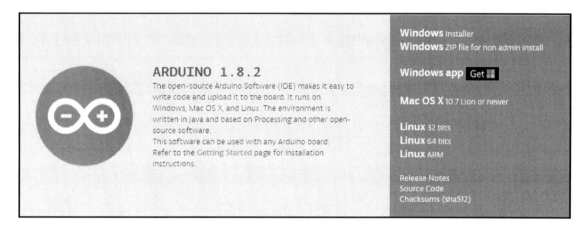

Now, you can download the version you want depending on your operating system. There are versions for Windows with and without admin rights, macOS X, and Linux for 32 bits, 64 bits, or ARM processors so that you can install and work, even on a Raspberry Pi.

After you have downloaded the Arduino IDE, you need to install it on your local computer.

If you are on Linux, you need to use the `xz` and `tar` command to open the Arduino IDE archive, then you can go into Arduino-1.8.2 and start it with `sudo ./arduino`.

In Windows, just launch the Arduino executable file, as follows:

Congratulations! You have installed the Arduino IDE and now it is time to configure it for ESP8266.

Configure Arduino IDE

To configure the Arduino IDE for ESP8266 you need to go to **File | Preferences**. The initial screen looks as follows:

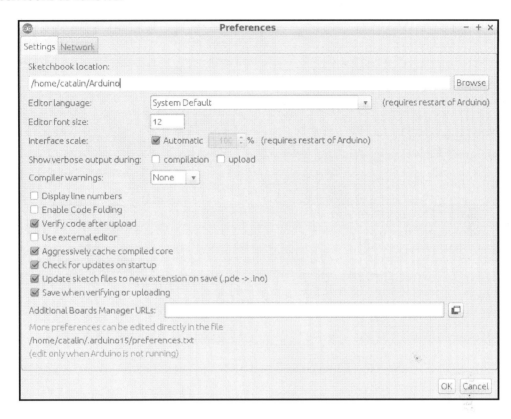

In this screen, you can customize some fields as follows:

- **Sketchbook location**: Here you can choose where your project files are stored.
- **Editor language**: If you prefer another language to the default one, you can change this field here; but after this, you need to restart the IDE.
- **Editor font size**: This is the font size used in the IDE.
- **Show verbose output during: compilation** and **upload**: I suggest you check both of them to have a detailed output during compilation, where you can see files and their paths and also the upload.
- **Display line numbers**: This field is good to see the line number in the right part of your IDE number.

- **Enable Code Folding**: This field gives you more space on the screen.
- **Additional Boards Manager URLs**: Here is the field that allows us to get and install the ESP8266 Xtensagcc compiler, required tools to flash the obtained firmware into the ESP8266 flash memory along with other board types. In this field, you need to add `http://arduino.esp8266.com/stable/package_esp8266com_index.json` and the **Preferences** screen will look as follows:

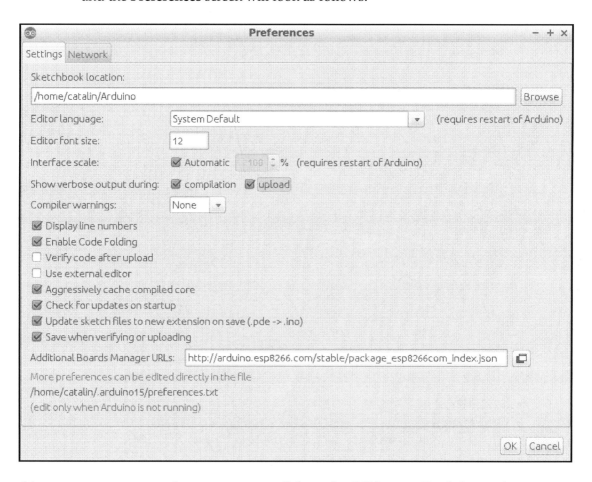

After you set up your preferences, you can click on the **OK** button. Don't forget that you are behind a proxy server; you need to fill in the details required in the **Network** tab.

Installing the ESP8266 SDK

After the preferences have been configured, now it is time to actually get the ESP8266 SDK and tools.

For this, you need to go to the following path and follow these steps:

1. Go to **Tools** | **Board: "Arduino/Genuino Uno"** | **Boards Manager...** :

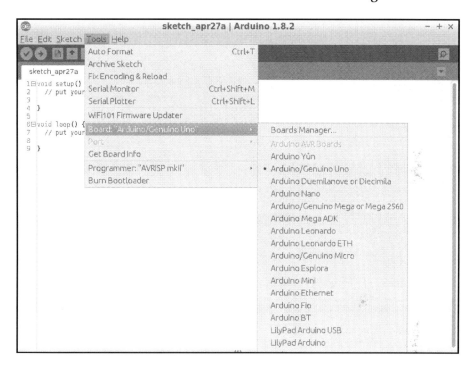

2. Subsequently, the **Boards Manager** will be opened.

3. Go to the end of the list and select the ESP8266 board and click on **Install**:

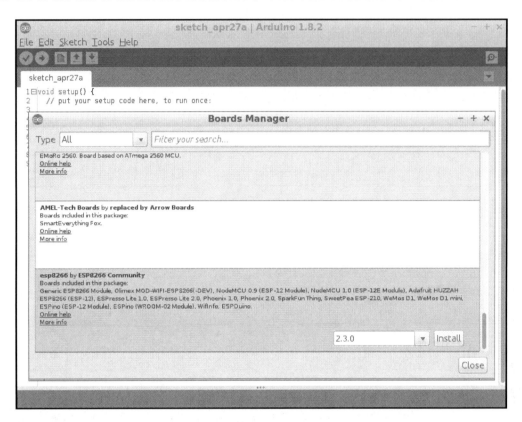

4. Now, depending on your internet connection, this can take some time. Sit back and relax, you are about to enter into the IoT world.

5. Look for the **INSTALLED** message, as in this picture:

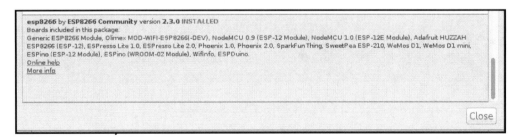

6. Now, go back to **Tools | Board: "Arduino/Genuino Uno"** and you should see a lot of ESP8266-based boards in the lower section:

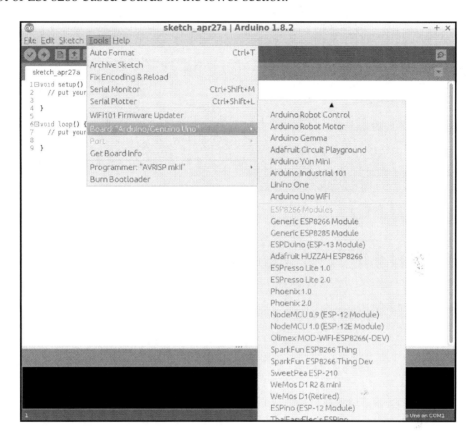

7. Select **NodeMCU 1.0 (ESP-12E Module)** and go back to the **Tools** menu, where you will see other configurations that you can perform for ESP8266:

   - **CPU Frequency: "80 MHz"**: This can be changed from **80 MHz** to **160 MHz**
   - The memory size of your module and the size of SPIFFS (1 or 3 MiB)

- The upload speed for the UART interface between your computer and the ESP8266 module. Select from **Upload Speed: "115200"** so that the binary file will be flashed 8 times faster than the default value of **115200**:

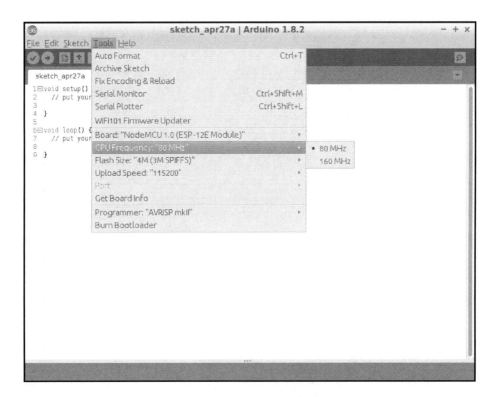

8. If you now have a module, you can connect it to your computer. Going again to **Tools** menu now, you will see this from the **Port** menu and you can go and select your serial interface connected to the ESP8266 module. For Linux, you can select /dev/ttyUSB0 and for Windows, one of your *COM* ports.

Before starting any program, let's look at the IDE buttons:

Let's start from left to right:

- Verify: This allows you to compile and check your code for errors
- Upload: This does what Verify does plus uploads generated firmware into ESP8266's flash memory
- New: This opens a new window so that you can create another program
- Open: This opens an existing program from your local disk
- Save: This saves your files on the disk
- Serial Monitor: This opens a window where you will be able to see and debug what you add into your program

How to install a library

In some chapters of this book, different libraries are needed; so let's see how a library can be installed.

The installed SDK has some basic libraries, but for sure, you will need more libraries to read various sensors, to parse JSON data, or to send MQTT messages. For the libraries that are referenced in the SDK repository, you just need to install them but for those that are not, you need to install them manually.

Libraries from the Arduino's repository

Some libraries exist in the official repository and you can install them in the following steps:

1. If it exists, then just go to **Sketch** | **Include Library** | **Manage Libraries**:

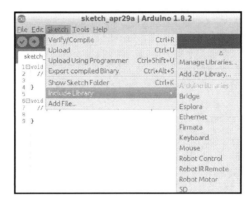

2. In a new window, delete the "**Filter your search...**" and write `Arduino Json`. The Arduino IDE will then search this library for you and if it has found it, you will be able to install it by clicking on it. You can also use this menu for updating a previously installed library or to change between versions of a library:

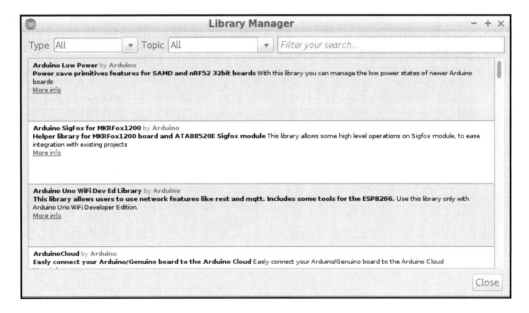

3. After the library is installed, you will see the following screen:

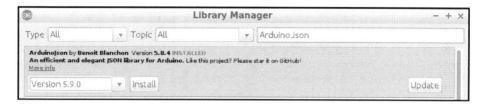

As an exercise, do the same for WiFiManager and PubSubClient libraries.

Library is not in the repository

Sometimes the library you need may not exist in the official repository but you may have found it on http://github.com as a ZIP archive.

To install the library, in this case, you need to perform the following steps:

1. Download the ZIP file and install it manually. For this, go to **Sketch|Include Library|Add .ZIP Library...** and select the downloaded library from your disk and press **Open**.
2. Include an existing library.
3. To include an existing library, go to **Sketch | Include Library** and select the library you want to include in your sketch.
4. The .h file will be added to your sketch and now you have access to the function a in this library to use them in your own program:

```
#include <ESP8266HTTPClient.h>

void setup() {
    // put your setup code here, to run once:

}

void loop() {
    // put your main code here, to run repeatedly:

}
```

It is time for your first program

To begin this, let's evaluate the basic input and output of the Witty ESP8266 module.

The definition of pins is **Light Dependent Resistor (LDR)** on Witty and is attached to A0 (the analog input), the push button is connected to GPIO 4, and the LEDs are connected to GPIO 12, GPIO 13, and GPIO 15:

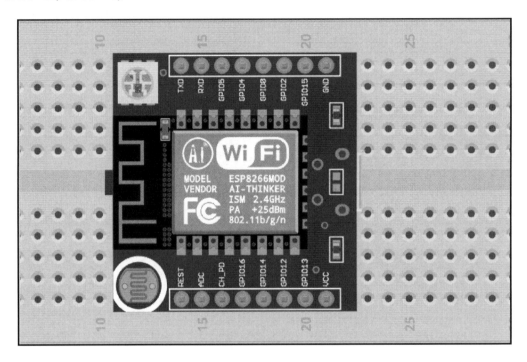

Delete everything that is in your Arduino IDE and replace it with the following code:

```
#define LDR      A0
#define BUTTON   4
#define RED      15
#define GREEN    12
#define BLUE     13
```

The setup section will run only once after the module is reset or powered. The serial UART is started with 115200 bps, so the messages can be seen in the Serial Monitor window, where you also need to set the same speed in the lower-right corner of the window; otherwise, weird characters will be seen.

All pins are defined as INPUT or OUTPUT depending on their usage. The button and LDR are configured as input pins and all LED connected pins are set as output:

```
void setup()
{
Serial.begin(115200);

pinMode(LDR, INPUT);
pinMode(BUTTON, INPUT);
pinMode(RED, OUTPUT);
pinMode(GREEN, OUTPUT);
pinMode(BLUE, OUTPUT);
}
```

The loop() function is continuously running after the setup() and, in it:

1. The analogRead function reads the value of the ambient light provided as 0-1 V by the LDR.
2. The digitalRead function reads the value of GPIO 4, that can be either 0 V when the button is pressed or VCC 3.3 V if the button is not pressed.
3. Show the data to the Serial Monitor with the Serial.print function. Serial.println just adds a new line.
4. Write a random value between 0 and 1023 to GPIO 15 and GPIO 12 that will control the red and green LED color intensity. This is **Pulse Width Modulation (PWM)**.
5. Turn on the blue LED connected to GPIO 13.
6. Wait 1000 ms (one second).
7. Turn off the blue LED and continue from step 1:

```
void loop()
{
Serial.print("LDR: ");
Serial.println(analogRead(LDR));
Serial.print("BUTTON: ");
Serial.println(digitalRead(BUTTON));

analogWrite(RED,    random(0,1023));
analogWrite(GREEN,  random(0,1023));
digitalWrite(BLUE, HIGH);
delay(1000);
digitalWrite(BLUE, LOW);
}
```

In order to compile and flush the binary into the ESP8266 chip you need to press the **Upload** button.

Seeing the result

In the Serial Monitor output, as shown in the following image, we can see the values for the ambient light and the status of the button, where 0 means pressed and 1 means not pressed:

If you don't have a Witty module, you will need some extra parts such as resistors, LED, push buttons, and LDR sensors, according to the following schematics:

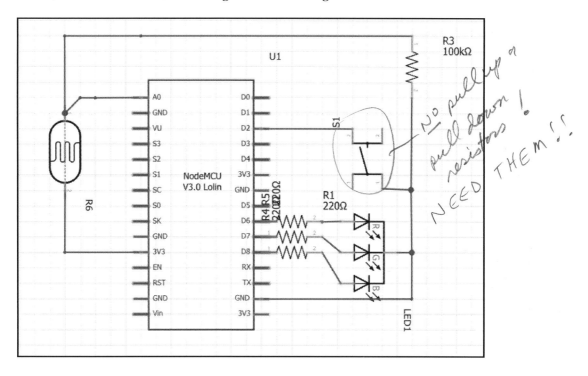

Let's review now the functions that allow you to control GPIO pins and the function that will print values in the Serial Monitor:

- `analogRead(pin)`: This reads the value on the **A0** pin
- `digitalRead(pin)`: This reads the value for a specified pin, either LOW or HIGH
- `digitalWrite(pin, value)`: This writes a LOW or HIGH value to a digital pin
- `Serial.println (val)`: This prints data to a serial port as human-readable ASCII characters ending with \r and a new line character \n

 Using `analogWrite(val)`, where val can be in the 0 to 1023 interval, a PWM digital output pin will have a voltage between 0 and 3.3V in 1023 steps.

Connecting ESP8266 to Wi-Fi

Until now, you have installed and configured the Arduino IDE for ESP8266 and learned how to control a LED, read an analog input, and dim a LED.

Now it is time to connect ESP8266 to Wi-Fi. Include ESP8266's Wi-Fi library and set up the SSID name and the Wi-Fi password:

```
#include <ESP8266WiFi.h>
const char* ssid     = "your_wifi_name";
const char* password = "your_wifi_password";
```

In the setup section, `Serial` is started and configured to send data at 115200 bps; a 10 ms delay is added to allow `Serial` to finish and the GPIO from 12 to 15 are configured as output and their value is set to LOW:

```
void setup() {
Serial.begin(115200);
delay(10);
pinMode(12, OUTPUT);
pinMode(13, OUTPUT);
pinMode(14, OUTPUT);
pinMode(15, OUTPUT);

digitalWrite(12,LOW);
digitalWrite(13,LOW);
digitalWrite(14,LOW);
digitalWrite(15,LOW);
```

We will start by connecting to a Wi-Fi network:

```
Serial.println();
Serial.println();
Serial.print("Connecting to ");
Serial.println(ssid);

WiFi.begin(ssid, password);
```

We wait until the status indicates that ESP8266 is connected to the Wi-Fi network. After this, the Wi-Fi connected message is displayed along with the IP address assigned to it by the router. Your router needs to be DHCP capable and have the DHCP feature enabled:

```
while (WiFi.status() != WL_CONNECTED) {
delay(500);
Serial.print(".");
  }

Serial.println("");
Serial.println("WiFi connected");
Serial.println("IP address: ");
Serial.println(WiFi.localIP());
}
```

In the loop section, the code checks to see whether the chip is connected to Wi-Fi and if this is true, the green LED will light on the Witty module:

```
void loop()
{
if(WiFi.status() == WL_CONNECTED)
digitalWrite(12, HIGH);
}
```

 As an exercise, you can light the RED led if there is no connectivity to your router, and the green LED otherwise.

The Serial Monitor will show the IP address assigned by the router, as follows:

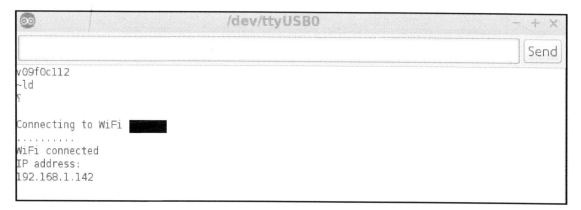

Getting data from the internet

Now that we have connected ESP8266 to the Wi-Fi network, we can receive and send data on the internet. More than this, we can read data from the input or from the sensors attached to the board and send their values to the internet.

First, let's read some data and what is more interesting than the current weather data? Let's create an account on `http://www.wunderground.com` and then, go to `https://www.wunderground.com/weather/api/d/pricing.htm`, where you will purchase a key for $0, as shown in the following image. After filling some data about the project, you will have your key:

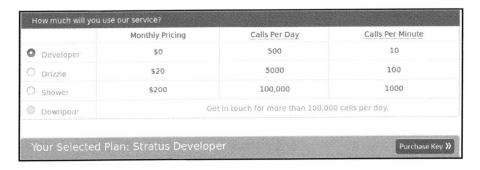

As you can see, with the developer key, you have 10 limited calls per minute that means you can get data every 6 seconds. Later in the code, we will get the data every 10 seconds.

To check your `API_KEY`, use it in a browser and check that you get any data. Replace `APY_KEY` with your own key:

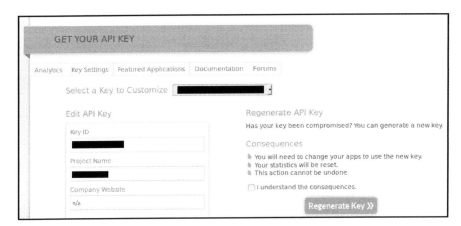

After this if you navigate to this link in your browser, `http://api.wunderground.com/api/APY_KEY/conditions/q/NL/Eindhoven.json`; you will get the following JSON formatted response from the `wunderground.com` server:

```
api.wunderground.com/api/ADD_APY_KEY_HERE/conditions/q/NL/Eindhoven.json

{
  "response": {
  "version":"0.1",
  "termsofService":"http://www.wunderground.com/weather/api/d/terms.html",
  "features": {
  "conditions": 1
  }
       }
  ,      "current_observation": {
            "image": {
            "url":"http://icons.wxug.com/graphics/wu2/logo_130x80.png",
            "title":"Weather Underground",
            "link":"http://www.wunderground.com"
            },
            "display_location": {
            "full":"Eindhoven, Netherlands",
            "city":"Eindhoven",
            "state":"NB",
            "state_name":"Netherlands",
            "country":"NL",
            "country_iso3166":"NL",
            "zip":"00000",
            "magic":"1",
            "wmo":"06370",
            "latitude":"51.43999863",
            "longitude":"5.48000002",
            "elevation":"20.1"
            },
            "observation_location": {
            "full":"Eindhoven, Villapark, NB",
            "city":"Eindhoven, Villapark",
            "state":"NB",
            "country":"NL",
            "country_iso3166":"NL",
```

Include the `ESP8266WiFi` library and the `ESP8266HTTPClient` library that will allow you to do an `HTTP GET` action to get the same JSON formatted message like you get using a browser:

```
#include <ESP8266WiFi.h>
#include <ESP8266HTTPClient.h>
```

Declare the SSID and the password of your Wi-Fi network:

```
const char* ssid     = "Your_WiFi_Name";
const char* password = "Your_WiFi_Password";

const String WUNDERGROUND_API_KEY = "YOUR_Wunderground_API_KEY";
const String WUNDERGROUND_COUNTRY = "NL";
const String WUNDERGROUND_CITY = "Eindhoven";
```

Construct the URL that will be used to get the data:

```
const String dataURL =
"http://api.wunderground.com/api/"+WUNDERGROUND_API_KEY+"/conditions/q/"+WU
NDERGROUND_COUNTRY+"/"+WUNDERGROUND_CITY+".json";
```

As usual, in the setup section, we will connect to the Wi-Fi network:

```
void setup() {
Serial.begin(115200);
delay(10);
Serial.println();
Serial.println();
Serial.print("Connecting to ");
Serial.println(ssid);

WiFi.begin(ssid, password);

while (WiFi.status() != WL_CONNECTED) {
delay(500);
Serial.print(".");
  }

Serial.println("");
Serial.println("WiFi connected");
Serial.println("IP address: ");
Serial.println(WiFi.localIP());


}
```

In the loop, if the Wi-Fi status is connected, then you will instantiate an HTTPClient object named http and start getting data every 10 seconds from the previously constructed link. In the payload variable, you will have the entire response from the server:

```
void loop()
{
if(WiFi.status() == WL_CONNECTED)
  {
HTTPClient http;
http.begin(dataURL);
inthttpCode = http.GET();

if(httpCode> 0) {
            // HTTP header has been send and Server response header has
been handled
Serial.printf("[HTTP] GET... code: %d\n", httpCode);

            // file found at server
```

```
if(httpCode == HTTP_CODE_OK) {
              String payload = http.getString();
Serial.println(payload);
        }
      }
  }
delay(10000);
}
```

If getting data every 10 seconds is too often, let's change it to once a minute by replacing the delay(10000) call that is blocking other code executions.

So, after const String WUNDERGROUND_CITY = "Eindhoven";, add two lines of code:

```
const long interval = 60 * 1000;
unsigned long previousMillis = 0;
```

Now, the loop function will change as follows:

```
void loop()
{
unsigned long currentMillis = millis();
if(currentMillis - previousMillis >= interval)
  {
previousMillis = currentMillis;
if(WiFi.status() == WL_CONNECTED)
    {
HTTPClient http;
http.begin(dataURL);
inthttpCode = http.GET();

if(httpCode > 0) {
            // HTTP header has been send and Server response header has
been handled
Serial.printf("[HTTP] GET... code: %d\n", httpCode);

            // file found at server
if(httpCode == HTTP_CODE_OK) {
              String payload = http.getString();
Serial.println(payload);
            }
        }
    }
  }
}
```

Now, the Serial Monitor will show a huge JSON with all the information about the weather from temperature to humidity, wind speed, dew point and much more every minute, as follows:

But what if you want to get only some specific data from this JSON? Fortunately, there is a Wunderground library for this. To install it, go to **Sketch | Include Library | Manage Libraries** and search for ESP8266 Weather Station. After installing this library, you also need to install the Json Straming Parser library that will parse the received JSON. You can follow these steps:

1. Install the ESP8266 Weather Station library:

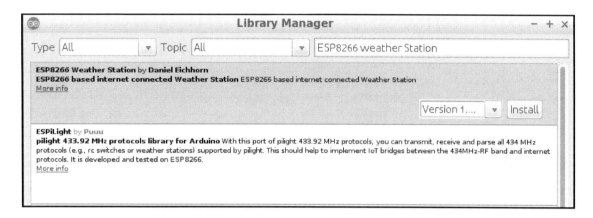

2. Also, install the JSON Streaming Parser library:

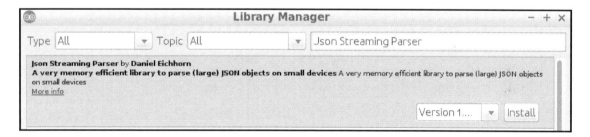

Now, let's get the same data, so the same API_KEY will be used but the data is parsed by library functions:

1. Include the headers' files for ESP8266 Wi-Fi.h, JSONListener.h, and WundergroundClient:

```
#include <ESP8266WiFi.h>
#include <JsonListener.h>
#include "WundergroundClient.h"
```

2. Define the `API_KEY` and set the metric Boolean variable:

```
const String  WUNDERGRROUND_API_KEY = "YOUR_API_KEY";
constboolean IS_METRIC = true;
```

3. Initialize `WundergoundClient` for the metric system:

```
WundergroundClientweather_data(IS_METRIC);
```

4. Also, initialize the Wi-Fi settings and constants used in getting the weather data:

```
const char* WIFI_SSID     = "YOUR_WIFI_SSID";
const char* WIFI_PASSWORD = "YOUR_WIFI_PASSWORD";
const String WUNDERGROUND_LANGUAGE = "EN";
const String WUNDERGROUND_COUNTRY = "NL";
const String WUNDERGROUND_CITY = "Eindhoven";
WiFiClientwifiClient;
```

5. Initialize the `setup` function to connect to the Wi-Fi network:

```
void setup() {
Serial.begin(115200);
delay(10);

WiFi.begin(WIFI_SSID, WIFI_PASSWORD);
delay(20);
Serial.print("Connecting to ");
Serial.println(WIFI_SSID);
while (WiFi.status() != WL_CONNECTED) {
delay(500);
Serial.print(".");
  }
Serial.println("");
Serial.println("WiFi connected!");
Serial.println();
}
```

6. In the `loop` function, get the data from the `wunderground.com` site every minute and show it in the Serial Monitor window:

```
void loop() {

if ((millis() % (60 * 1000)) == 0) {
Serial.println();
Serial.println("\n\nNext Loop-Step: " + String(millis()) + ":");

weather_data.updateConditions(WUNDERGRROUND_API_KEY,
WUNDERGROUND_LANGUAGE, WUNDERGROUND_COUNTRY, WUNDERGROUND_CITY);
```

```
Serial.println("wundergroundHours: " + weather_data.getHours());
Serial.println("wundergroundMinutes: " +
weather_data.getMinutes());
Serial.println("wundergroundSeconds: " +
weather_data.getSeconds());
Serial.println("wundergroundDate: " + weather_data.getDate());

Serial.println("wundergroundMoonPctIlum: " +
weather_data.getMoonPctIlum());
Serial.println("wundergroundMoonAge: " +
weather_data.getMoonAge());
Serial.println("wundergroundMoonPhase: " +
weather_data.getMoonPhase());
Serial.println("wundergroundSunriseTime: " +
weather_data.getSunriseTime());
Serial.println("wundergroundSunsetTime: " +
weather_data.getSunsetTime());
Serial.println("wundergroundMoonriseTime: " +
weather_data.getMoonriseTime());
Serial.println("wundergroundMoonsetTime: " +
weather_data.getMoonsetTime());
Serial.println("wundergroundWindSpeed: " +
weather_data.getWindSpeed());
Serial.println("wundergroundWindDir: " +
weather_data.getWindDir());

Serial.println("wundergroundCurrentTemp: " +
weather_data.getCurrentTemp());
Serial.println("wundergroundTodayIcon: " +
weather_data.getTodayIcon());
Serial.println("wundergroundTodayIconText: " +
weather_data.getTodayIconText());
Serial.println("wundergroundMeteoconIcon: " +
weather_data.getMeteoconIcon(weather_data.getTodayIconText()));
Serial.println("wundergroundWeatherText: " +
weather_data.getWeatherText());
Serial.println("wundergroundHumidity: " +
weather_data.getHumidity());
Serial.println("wundergroundPressure: " +
weather_data.getPressure());
Serial.println("wundergroundDewPoint: " +
weather_data.getDewPoint());
Serial.println("wundergroundPrecipitationToday: " +
weather_data.getPrecipitationToday());

Serial.println();
Serial.println("-------------------------------------------------
/\n");
```

```
        }
      }
```

7. The output for the Serial Monitor is as follows:

Now, as an exercise, you can read the temperature and turn on or off an LED' if there are icing conditions or humidity and the temperature is too high outside.

Sending data to the internet

Now, let's send the same data to the internet. The first thing to do is to create an account on http://thingspeak.com and set up a channel. Each channel has eight fields that you can use to store the data transmitted by ESP8266.

As a free account, you need not send data more often than three times per minute. The advantage is that your data is stored on their server and you can see them on a nice graphic or embed them as an IFRAME in another web server.

In **Channel Settings**, create one field and name it **Light**, then go to the API key tab and get Write API KEY. Here, you can also define a read APY KEY if you have an application that wants to read data written by other modules. It is a rudimentary way of sharing data between modules.

Since the Witty module has the LDR, let's use it to log the data every minute on api.thingspeak.com:

```
#include <ESP8266WiFi.h>

const char* WIFI_SSID     = "YOUR_WIFI_SSID";
const char* WIFI_PASSWORD = "YOUR WIFI_PASSWORD";
const char* host = "api.thingspeak.com";
const char* writeAPIKey = "YOUR_WRITE_API_KEY";

#define LDR      A0
```

In the setup() function, which is executed once, the LDR pin is set as an INPUT pin and will connect the ESP8266 to the Wi-Fi network with the WiFi.begin(WIFI_SSID, WIFI_PASSWORD) function:

```
void setup()
{
Serial.begin(115200);
delay(10);
pinMode(LDR, INPUT);
WiFi.begin(WIFI_SSID, WIFI_PASSWORD);
delay(20);
Serial.print("Connecting to ");
```

```
Serial.println(WIFI_SSID);
while (WiFi.status() != WL_CONNECTED) {
delay(500);
Serial.print(".");
  }
Serial.println("");
Serial.println("WiFi connected!");
Serial.println();
}
```

In the `loop()` function every minute the light intensity will be read from the LDR sensor and post it on the `Light` field on a channel from `https://thingspeak.com/`:

```
void loop()
{
if ((millis() % (60 * 1000)) == 0) {
// make TCP connections
WiFiClient client;
const  int httpPort = 80;
if (!client.connect(host, httpPort)) {
return;
  }

  String url = "/update?key=";
url+=writeAPIKey;
url+="&field1=";
url+=String(analogRead(LDR));
url+="\r\n";
Serial.println(url);
  // Request to the server
client.print(String("GET ") + url + " HTTP/1.1\r\n" +
               "Host: " + host + "\r\n" +
               "Connection: close\r\n\r\n");
  }

}
```

Let's see how the data looks after a few minutes:

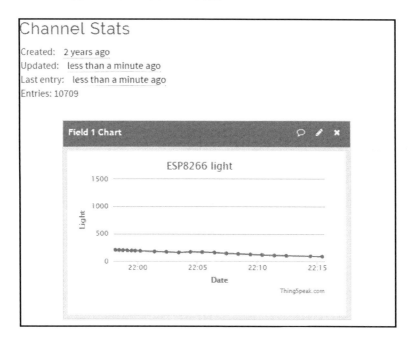

Now, let's combine the sketches that read the weather from `wunderground.com` and this one that sends data to `thingspeak.com`. It will take the temperature, humidity, dew point, and precipitation and it will store them on `thinkspeak.com` so that later we can import them. Basically, this will be a weather logger:

```
#include <ESP8266WiFi.h>
#include <JsonListener.h>
#include "WundergroundClient.h"
```

The following are the Wunderground settings:

```
const String  WUNDERGRROUND_API_KEY = "58dfbeb30d02af26";
const Boolean IS_METRIC = true;
WundergroundClient weather_data(IS_METRIC);
const char* WIFI_SSID      = "YOUR_WIFI_SSID";
const char* WIFI_PASSWORD = "YOUR_WIFI_PASSWORD";
const String WUNDERGROUND_LANGUAGE = "EN";
const String WUNDERGROUND_COUNTRY = "NL";
const String WUNDERGROUND_CITY = "Eindhoven";
const char* host = "api.thingspeak.com";
const char* writeAPIKey = "YOUR_WRITE_API_KEY";
WiFiClient wifiClient
```

The following is the `setup()` function to connect to the Wi-Fi network:

```
void setup() {

Serial.begin(115200);
delay(10);

WiFi.begin(WIFI_SSID, WIFI_PASSWORD);
delay(20);
Serial.print("Connecting to ");
Serial.println(WIFI_SSID);
while (WiFi.status() != WL_CONNECTED) {
delay(500);
Serial.print(".");
  }
Serial.println("");
Serial.println("WiFi connected!");
Serial.println();
}
```

In the `loop()` function, every minute weather data will be retrieved from
`wunderground.com` and it will post it to `thingspeak.com`. Along with the temperature,
pressure, precipitation and dew point more information will be printed in the serial output
like moon phase, sunrise or sunset, information that can be used if you plan to add a
display module to visualize all weather conditions:

```
void loop() {
if ((millis() % (60 * 1000)) == 0) {
Serial.println();
Serial.println("\n\nNext Loop-Step: " + String(millis()) + ":");

weather_data.updateConditions(WUNDERGRROUND_API_KEY, WUNDERGROUND_LANGUAGE,
WUNDERGROUND_COUNTRY, WUNDERGROUND_CITY);

Serial.println("wundergroundHours: " + weather_data.getHours());
Serial.println("wundergroundMinutes: " + weather_data.getMinutes());
Serial.println("wundergroundSeconds: " + weather_data.getSeconds());
Serial.println("wundergroundDate: " + weather_data.getDate());

Serial.println("wundergroundMoonPctIlum: " +
weather_data.getMoonPctIlum());
Serial.println("wundergroundMoonAge: " + weather_data.getMoonAge());
Serial.println("wundergroundMoonPhase: " + weather_data.getMoonPhase());
Serial.println("wundergroundSunriseTime: " +
weather_data.getSunriseTime());
Serial.println("wundergroundSunsetTime: " + weather_data.getSunsetTime());
Serial.println("wundergroundMoonriseTime: " +
```

```
weather_data.getMoonriseTime());
Serial.println("wundergroundMoonsetTime: " +
weather_data.getMoonsetTime());
Serial.println("wundergroundWindSpeed: " + weather_data.getWindSpeed());
Serial.println("wundergroundWindDir: " + weather_data.getWindDir());

Serial.println("wundergroundCurrentTemp: " +
weather_data.getCurrentTemp());
Serial.println("wundergroundTodayIcon: " + weather_data.getTodayIcon());
Serial.println("wundergroundTodayIconText: " +
weather_data.getTodayIconText());
Serial.println("wundergroundMeteoconIcon: " +
weather_data.getMeteoconIcon(weather_data.getTodayIconText()));
Serial.println("wundergroundWeatherText: " +
weather_data.getWeatherText());
Serial.println("wundergroundHumidity: " + weather_data.getHumidity());
Serial.println("wundergroundPressure: " + weather_data.getPressure());
Serial.println("wundergroundDewPoint: " + weather_data.getDewPoint());
Serial.println("wundergroundPrecipitationToday: " +
weather_data.getPrecipitationToday());

WiFiClient client;
const int httpPort = 80;
if (!client.connect(host, httpPort)) {
return;
    }

    String url = "/update?key=";
url+=writeAPIKey;
url+="&field1=";
url+=String(weather_data.getCurrentTemp());
url+="&field2=";
url+=String(weather_data.getPressure());
url+="&field3=";
url+=String(weather_data.getDewPoint());
url+="&field4=";
url+=String(weather_data.getPrecipitationToday());
url+="\r\n";
Serial.println(url);
    // Request to the server
client.print(String("GET ") + url + " HTTP/1.1\r\n" +
                "Host: " + host + "\r\n" +
                "Connection: close\r\n\r\n");

Serial.println("-----------------------------------------------/\n");
  }
}
```

After a few minutes, you can see the values received by the ESP8266 from `wunderground.com` and posted on `thingspeak.com` displayed on four graphs:

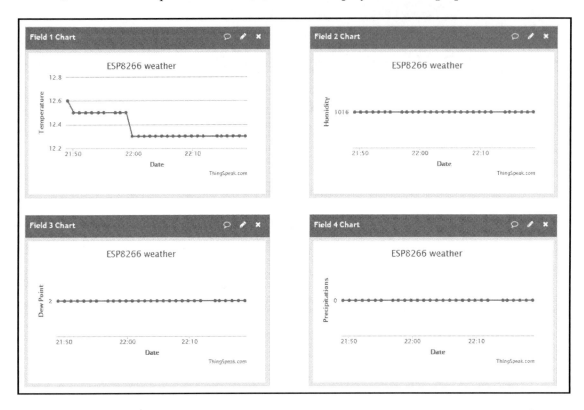

Summary

The first step in developing IoT applications has been completed. Now, you have the knowledge for installing and configuring the Arduino IDE for the ESP8266 development, and on how to transmit and receive data, to and from the internet. The next step will be to make the ESP8266 modules talk to each other, no matter where they are located.

Building and Configuring Your Own MQTT Server

2

Now that you have learned how to use analog and digital outputs, to send and receive data via Wi-Fi, it is time to move on the next part where you will discover the MQTT protocol and how to use it.

In the previous chapter the ESP8266 was only communicating with servers: in this chapter, we will see how ESP8266 modules can communicate with each other through **Message Queue Telemetry Transport** (**MQTT**).

Message Queue Telemetry Transport

Usually, end devices have a limited memory and CPU power, running on batteries, so connecting them with servers requires a light protocol. Enter MQTT, which was invented in 1999 by Andy Stanford-Clark from IBM and Arlen Nipper from Arcom, a SCADA protocol design initially for battery operated devices to supervise oil pipelines. Later in 2010, IBM released it as a royalty-free protocol. In 2014, OASIS announced that the MQTT v.3.1.1 had become an OASIS standard and a lot of MQTT clients were developed for all programming languages.

The characteristics of MQTT are listed as follows:

- **Data agnostic**: MQTT can transport all kind of data, from sensor data to images or over the air updates
- **Lightweight and bandwidth efficient**: Smallest frame is only 2 bytes long

- **Provide QoS**: Three **Quality of Service (QoS)** levels
- Runs on top of the TCP/IP stack
- **Simple to develop**: Clients exist for all operating systems and programming languages
- **Central broker**: Can connect different devices without having to worry about compatibility
- **Session awareness**: Provides an identity-based approach for subscriptions
- Flexible subscription topics

Quality of service

The MQTT standard defines three QoS levels:

- QoS 0: At most once, a message with QoS 0 will be sent once by the client and will not be stored or responded to. Use this QoS if your application can afford to lose a packet once in a while. For example, if you are sending the temperature every second and one packet is lost, there will be no problem since the temperature didn't change in one second.
- QoS 1: A least once, If you need a confirmation that your message arrived at its destination, then send it with QoS 1. In this case, the broker is storing the message until it receives a response from the other client. For example, if your message needs to open a relay that is starting an air fan or a lamp, you need to be sure that the message arrived at a destination.
- QoS 2: Exactly once, if you have an application that needs to receive messages only once and doesn't allow duplicates use QoS 2 for your message.

Security

MQTT is a protocol that is running over the TCP/IP so you can use it to encrypt the data with TLS/SSL and to have a secure connection between clients.

Retain messages and last will

Let's imagine that we need to build a module that will send the temperature and humidity every hour to the server and must run on batteries. Because the data is not sent very often and is running on batteries the module will be put into deep sleep between the sendings. At a certain point in time if the data is requested every five minutes there is no way to tell the module to change its update time other than using a **retain message**. From the web application, a retain message will be sent and the broker will send that message when the module transmits for the first time. In this way, when the module wakes up and subscribes to the server on a configuration topic, the broker will deliver the new update interval. The message is parsed by the module and from now on will wake up and will transmit every five minutes instead of every hour.

When you have a use case for an application that depends on some critical values sent by a sensor, then you can detect when a client has stopped transmitting or loses its power by using the **last will**. When the client is connecting to the broker it will also specify the last will topic and its last message. For example, if there is a network failure on the client or it is not responding to Keep Alive messages, then the broker will send to all clients that subscribed to the last will topic, a message from that client. Usually, the Last Will message is used together with the Retain Message option.

Basic terminology

Until now terms such as a central broker, topic, publish, subscribe terms have been used, so it is time to explain them using an analogy with a post office and the messages are newspapers or magazines:

- **Broker**: It is a software application (postal office) that receives messages (magazines) from clients (editors), and routes the messages according to the subscriber's requests.
- **Client**: It is a device that can publish a message (magazine) or can receive a message (magazine) or both.
- **Topic**: It is a string (magazine) that is used by the broker to filter messages for each connected clients. It is sent by clients to the broker in a subscribe request to express the desire in receiving messages published by other clients. It is sent by the clients when publishing messages to any other client that subscribed on the same topic.

- **Publish**: Action of sending a message (magazine) to another client on a specific topic.
- **Subscribe**: Action of informing the broker about an interest in receiving future messages published by other clients on that topic. A client can subscribe to multiple topics.
- **Unsubscribe**: Action of a client that is telling the broker not to send messages to the specified topic.

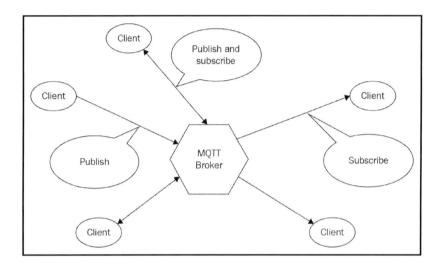

MQTT Architecture

Since one characteristic of MQTT is *flexible subscription topics*, let's see how a topic is formed. Topics consist of a hierarchical level using a / as a topic level separator.

Here are examples of valid topics:

- `Europe/France/Paris/temperature`
- `62/livingroom/temperature`
- `456733-a55h56-667743/battery`

Topics are case-sensitive so `Europe/France/Paris/temperature` is different than `europe/France/Paris/temperature`.

Wildcards on topics

If publishing data to another client through the broker it is necessary to specify the full topic name: for receiving messages clients can subscribe using the wildcard level for topics. Wildcards are single level + and multi-level #:

1. Single-level +.
2. Using the + in the subscription level for a topic means that instead of + can be any value.
3. If you want to build a display panel to show the temperature from your house, you build modules that read the temperature from every room and publish it on topics such as:

   ```
   myHouse/groundFloor/livingroom/temperature
   myHouse/groundFloor/kitchen/temperature
   ```

4. `myHouse/firstFloor/bedroom/temperature` and the display module will subscribe to:

   ```
   myHouse/groundFloor/+/temperature
   ```

5. Every time a temperature module located on the ground floor is publishing some message on its topic, the display module will receive it, so it is not necessary to subscribe on each topic, but it will not receive the data from the following topics:

   ```
   myHouse/groundFloor/livingroom/humidity
   myHouse/groundFloor/kitchen/light
   ```

6. Multi-level #.
7. Using # in the subscribed topic level client will receive all messages from that level down.
8. If the display panel is subscribing to topic.
9. `myHouse/groundFloor/#` that means that it will receive all the messages published on topics that start with `myHouse/groundFloor`.
10. If a client subscribes to #, the topic will receive all the messages published within that broker.
11. Special topics $.
12. If you want to monitor internal statistics of the broker then you need to subscribe to the `$SYS` topics.

13. Here are examples of what you can get:

```
$SYS/broker/clients/total
  7
  The total number of active and inactive clients currently connected and registered on the broker.
$SYS/broker/clients/inactive
  4
  Deprecated: The total number of persistent clients (with clean session disabled) that are registered at the broker but are currently disconnected.
$SYS/broker/clients/disconnected
  4
  The total number of persistent clients (with clean session disabled) that are registered at the broker but are currently disconnected.
$SYS/broker/clients/active
  3
  Deprecated: The number of currently connected clients.
$SYS/broker/clients/connected
  3
  The number of currently connected clients.
$SYS/broker/clients/maximum

  The maximum number of active clients that have been connected to the broker. This is only calculated when the $SYS topic tree is updated, so
  short lived client connections may not be counted.
$SYS/broker/clients/expired
  0
  The number of disconnected persistent clients that have been expired and removed through the persistent_client_expiration option
$SYS/broker/messages/stored
  1904
  The number of messages currently held in the message store. This includes retained messages and messages queued for durable clients.
$SYS/broker/messages/received
  1208818
  The total number of PUBLISH messages received since the broker started.
$SYS/broker/messages/sent
  654351
  The total number of PUBLISH messages sent since the broker started.
$SYS/broker/subscriptions/count
  10
  The total number of subscriptions active on the broker.
```

$SYS output example

Introducing Mosquitto broker

Eclipse Mosquitto™ is an open source MQTT broker that implements the MQTT v3.1 and MQTT v.3.1.1 standards and provides a lightweight method to transport messages, allowing publish and subscription for low power sensors, mobile devices, embedded computers, and micro controllers.

You can install Mosquitto on a Raspberry Pi or on AWS instance or on a VirtualBox Linux instance directly from your Linux repository distribution; or you can get the source code and compile it yourself if you want support from websockets.

Installing from your Linux distribution repository:

1. First upgrade to the latest version:

    ```
    sudo apt update && sudo apt upgrade
    ```

2. Then install `mosquito`:

    sudo apt install mosquitto

    You should see the following screen:

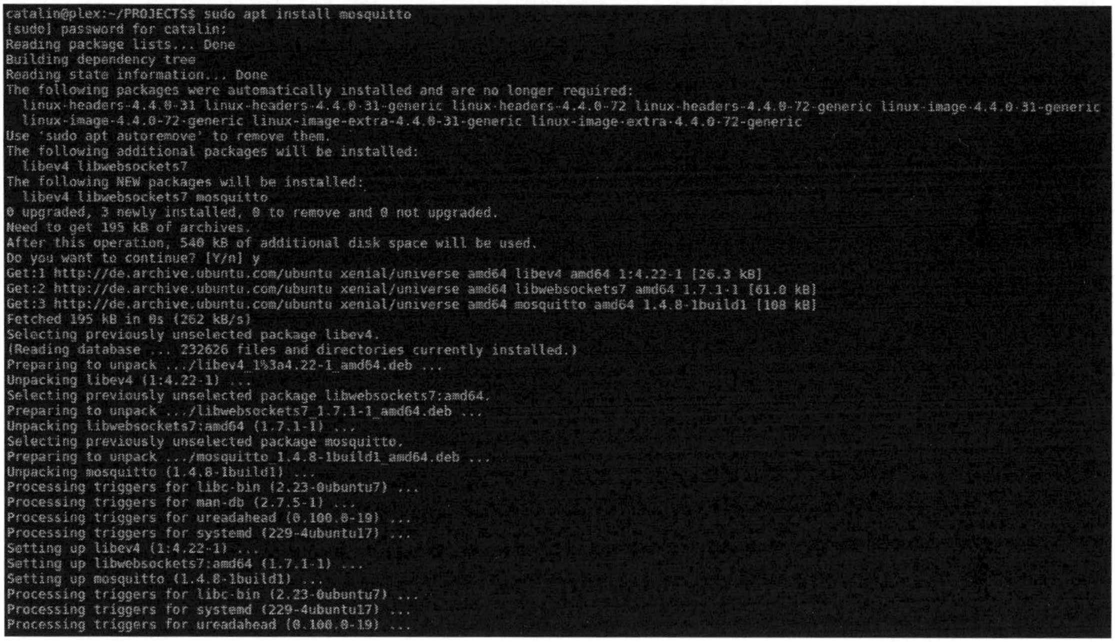

Installing Mosquitto

3. After installing the Mosquitto broker verify that the broker is started and install `mosquitto-clients` as follows:

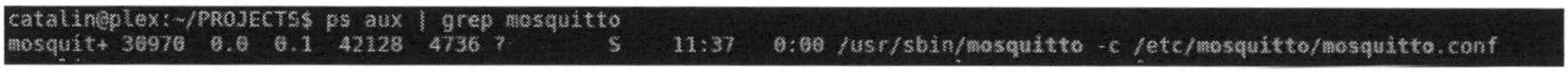

Verify if Mosquitto is running

4. Type the following command:

```
sudo apt install mosquitto-clients
```

You will get the following screen:

```
catalin@plex:~/PROJECTS$ sudo apt install mosquitto-clients
Reading package lists... Done
Building dependency tree
Reading state information... Done
The following packages were automatically installed and are no longer required:
  linux-headers-4.4.0-31 linux-headers-4.4.0-31-generic linux-headers-4.4.0-72 linux-headers-4.4.0-72-generic linux-image-4.4.0-31-generic
  linux-image-4.4.0-72-generic linux-image-extra-4.4.0-31-generic linux-image-extra-4.4.0-72-generic
Use 'sudo apt autoremove' to remove them.
The following additional packages will be installed:
  libc-ares2 libmosquitto1
The following NEW packages will be installed:
  libc-ares2 libmosquitto1 mosquitto-clients
0 upgraded, 3 newly installed, 0 to remove and 0 not upgraded.
Need to get 96.2 kB of archives.
After this operation, 330 kB of additional disk space will be used.
Do you want to continue? [Y/n] y
Get:1 http://de.archive.ubuntu.com/ubuntu xenial-updates/main amd64 libc-ares2 amd64 1.10.0-3ubuntu0.1 [34.1 kB]
Get:2 http://de.archive.ubuntu.com/ubuntu xenial/universe amd64 libmosquitto1 amd64 1.4.8-1build1 [31.1 kB]
Get:3 http://de.archive.ubuntu.com/ubuntu xenial/universe amd64 mosquitto-clients amd64 1.4.8-1build1 [31.0 kB]
Fetched 96.2 kB in 0s (226 kB/s)
Selecting previously unselected package libc-ares2:amd64.
(Reading database ... 232666 files and directories currently installed.)
Preparing to unpack .../libc-ares2_1.10.0-3ubuntu0.1_amd64.deb ...
Unpacking libc-ares2:amd64 (1.10.0-3ubuntu0.1) ...
Selecting previously unselected package libmosquitto1:amd64.
Preparing to unpack .../libmosquitto1_1.4.8-1build1_amd64.deb ...
Unpacking libmosquitto1:amd64 (1.4.8-1build1) ...
Selecting previously unselected package mosquitto-clients.
Preparing to unpack .../mosquitto-clients_1.4.8-1build1_amd64.deb ...
Unpacking mosquitto-clients (1.4.8-1build1) ...
Processing triggers for libc-bin (2.23-0ubuntu7) ...
Processing triggers for man-db (2.7.5-1) ...
Setting up libc-ares2:amd64 (1.10.0-3ubuntu0.1) ...
Setting up libmosquitto1:amd64 (1.4.8-1build1) ...
Setting up mosquitto-clients (1.4.8-1build1) ...
Processing triggers for libc-bin (2.23-0ubuntu7) ...
```

Installing Mosquitto-clients

Mosquitto clients come with three very important utilities:

- `mosquitto_sub`: A simple mqtt client that will subscribe to a single topic and print all messages it receives
- `mosquitto_pub`: A simple mqtt client that will publish a message on a single topic and exit
- `mosquitto_passwd`: A tool for managing password files for Mosquitto

Using any of them with the `--help` options such as `mosquitto_sub --help` will give a comprehensive list with all the options you can use to test your broker.

After installation Mosquitto is started as a service and is listening on the port 1883. To test this initial installation let's subscribe to a topic and publish a message on that topic.

Subscribing to a topic using the -t option is shown in the following command:

```
mosquitto_sub -t livingroom/temperature
```

Run this command as follows:

```
catalin@plex:~/PROJECTS$ mosquitto_sub -t livingroom/temperature
```

Subscribing to a topic, **Observation**: This command assumes that the broker is running on the local server. When you deploy Mosquitto to an internet **Virtual Private Server** (**VPS**) for subscription add the -h to specify the IP address of your server instance (use ifconfig to find it) and also the port -p 1884 if you are not using the default 1883 port. In this case the command will be:

```
mosquitto_sub -h 46.102.34.87 -t livingroom/temperature
```

In another terminal let's publish some JSON-formatted message on the same topic livingroom/temperature. Use the following command a few times and see the messages:

```
mosquitto_pub -t livingroom/temperature -m {"t":27.4}
```

You should see the following output:

```
catalin@plex:~/PROJECTS$ mosquitto_sub -t livingroom/temperature
{t:27.4}
{t:27.4}
{t:27.4}
{t:27.4}
```

First data received on a topic

After sending the message mosquitto_pub will exit. If you want to send the value every second use the watch utility, where -n 1 is the number of seconds between the commands:

```
watch -n 1 mosquitto_pub -t livingroom/temperature -m {"t":27.4}
```

You can exercise now using the +, # on the subscribing topic `mosquitto_sub -t livingroom/#` will give you all the data that are sent with commands:

```
mosquitto_pub -t livingroom/temperature -m {"t":27.4}
mosquitto_pub -t livingroom/humidity -m {"h":68}
```

You should see the following:

```
catalin@plex:~/PROJECTS$ mosquitto_sub -t livingroom/#
{t:27.4}
{h:68}
```

Receiving data from different sensors

And the using of + in topics, subscribe to all temperature topics:

```
mosquitto_sub - t myhouse/+/temperature
```

And sending from other terminal messages such as:

```
mosquitto_pub -t myhouse/living/temperature -m {"t":25.6}
mosquitto_pub -t myhouse/kitchen/temperature -m {"t":27.1}
```

In the terminal where you subscribed you will see all the following messages:

```
catalin@plex:~$ mosquitto_sub -t myhouse/+/temperature
{t:25.6}
{t:27.1}
{t:25.6}
{t:27.1}
```

ESP8266 and MQTT

To use the ESP8266 as a client for sending data to a broker you will need a library that offers MQTT support. For this you can use the `PubSubClient` library, which can be installed like other libraries; see `Chapter 1`, *Getting Started with the ESP8266*:

1. Go to **Sketch** | **Include Library** | **Manage Libraries...**, as follows:

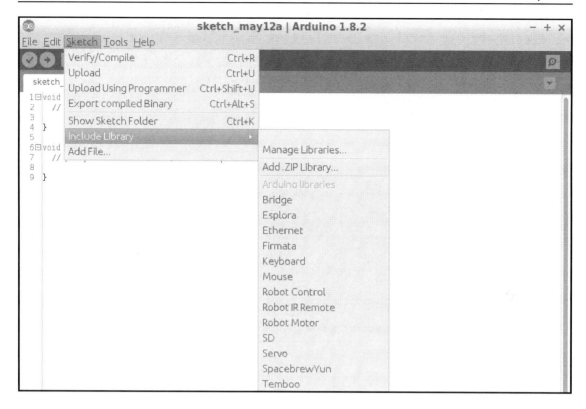

Manage libraries

2. And search for the `PubSubClient` library and click **Install** as in the following screenshot:

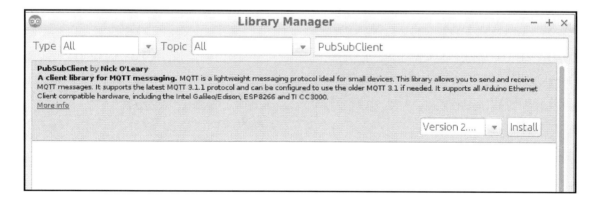

Publishing data from the ESP8266

Start a new sketch via **File** | **New** in the Arduino IDE and paste in the following code. Include the `ESP8266WiFi` library and the `PubSubClient` one:

```
#include <ESP8266WiFi.h>
#include <PubSubClient.h>
```

Update these with values suitable for your network. Use `ifconfig` to get the IP address of the server where the Mosquitto broker is installed. If your server has an FQDN name such as `myiotserver.com` and is registered into the DNS, then instead of the IP address in `mqtt_server` you can use the FQDN name:

```
const char* wifi_network = "YOUR_WIFI_SSID";
const char* wifi_pass = "YOUR_WIFI_PASSWORD";
const char* mqtt_serv_address = "192.168.1.116";
const int mqtt_port_number = 1883;
```

Instantiate a `WiFiClient` and pass it to the `PubSubClient`:

```
WiFiClient espClient;
PubSubClient client(espClient);
long lastMsg = 0;
char msg[50];
int value = 0;
```

The `setup()` function will start connecting the ESP8266 to the Wi-Fi network by calling the `setup_wifi()` function and set the MQTT server and port to be used via the `client.Setserver()` function:

```
void setup() {
Serial.begin(115200);
setup_wifi();
client.setServer(mqtt_serv_address, mqtt_port_number);
}

void setup_wifi() {

delay(10);
  // We start by connecting to a WiFi network
Serial.println();
Serial.print("Connecting to ");
Serial.println(wifi_network);

WiFi.begin(wifi_network, wifi_pass);

while (WiFi.status() != WL_CONNECTED) {
```

```
WiFi.begin(wifi_network, wifi_pass);

Serial.print(".");
delay(5000);
    }

Serial.println("");
Serial.println("WiFi connected");
Serial.println("IP address: ");
Serial.println(WiFi.localIP());
    }
```

If keep alive packets from the MQTT server to the ESP8266 module are lost and the communication is interrupted, the reconnect() function will try to connect again to the MQTT server. This reconnect function is also used as a first connection to the server.

After connecting to the MQTT server the ESP8266 will publish a message "Hello world, I am ESP8266!" on the fromEsp8266 topic:

```
void reconnect() {
  // Loop until we're reconnected
while (!client.connected()) {
Serial.print("Attempting MQTT connection...");
    // Attempt to connect
if (client.connect("ESP8266Client"))
    {
Serial.println("connected");
      // Once connected, publish an announcement...
client.publish("fromEsp8266", "Hello world, I am ESP8266!");
    } else {
Serial.print("failed, rc=");
Serial.print(client.state());
Serial.println(" try again in 5 seconds");
      // Wait 5 seconds before retrying
delay(5000);
    }
  }
}
```

The `loop` function will check for connectivity with the MQTT broker, reconnect to it if there is a problem with connection, and every two seconds will publish a message on the `fromEsp8266` topic:

```
void loop() {

if (!client.connected()) {
reconnect();
    }
client.loop();

long now = millis();
if (now - lastMsg> 2000) {
lastMsg = now;
      ++value;
snprintf (msg, 75, "Hello world #%ld", value);
Serial.print("Publish message: ");
Serial.println(msg);
client.publish("fromEsp8266", msg);
    }
}
```

After compiling and uploading the code to the ESP8266 module, in a terminal window subscribe to the `fromEsp8266` topic. The messages sent by the ESP8266 module will be shown in the terminal window:

```
catalin@plex:~$ mosquitto_sub -h 192.168.1.116 -t fromEsp8266
Hello world, I am ESP8266!
Hello world #1
Hello world #2
Hello world #3
Hello world #4
Hello world #5
Hello world #6
```

Messages published by ESP8266

Observation: Remember that topic names are case-sensitive. As an exercise you can send the pin status (HIGH or LOW) as was presented in Chapter 1, *Getting Started with the ESP8266.*

Use `digitalRead(PIN_NUMER)` instead of value.

Receiving MQTT messages in the ESP8266

Now let's publish a message using `mosquitto_pub` and receive it in the ESP8266.

For this the ESP8266 needs to subscribe to the same topic on which `mosquitto_pub` will publish the message. Let's call the topic `outdoor/light` and it will publish on 0 or 1 values. If the ESP8266 receives the value as 1, it will turn on a LED connected to GPIO 12 and if it will receives a 0, it will turn off that LED:

```
#include <ESP8266WiFi.h>
#include <PubSubClient.h>
```

Update these with values suitable for your network:

```
const char* wifi_network= "YOUR_WIFI_SSID";
const char* password = "YOUR_WIFI_PASSWORD";
const char* mqtt_serv_address = "YOUR_MQTT_SERVER_IP";
const int mqtt_port_number = 1883;
#define OUTDOOR_LIGHT   12

WiFiClient  espClient;
PubsubClient client(espClient);
long lastMsg; = 0;
```

Start the connection to the Wi-Fi network and set the name of the function that will be called when a message is received from the MQTT broker, as follows:

```
void setup() {
pinMode(OUTDOOR_LIGHT, OUTPUT);       // Initialize the BUILTIN_LED pin as an
output
Serial.begin(115200);
setup_wifi();
client.setServer(mqtt_serv_address, mqtt_port_number);
client.setCallback(callback);
}
```

Connect to the Wi-Fi network:

```
void setup_wifi() {
delay(10);
  // We start by connecting to a WiFi network
Serial.println();
Serial.print("Connecting to ");
Serial.println(wifi_network);

WiFi.begin(wifi_network, password);
```

```
while (WiFi.status() != WL_CONNECTED) {
WiFi.begin(wifi_network, password);

Serial.print(".");
delay(5000);
    }

Serial.println("");
Serial.println("WiFi connected");
Serial.println("IP address: ");
Serial.println(WiFi.localIP());
    }
```

When a message will arrive in the ESP8266 MQTT client the function that will be called is `callback()`, with parameters topic containing the name of the topic on which topic the message arrived, in case that module subscribed to multiple topics, the actual content of the message, and the length of the message:

```
void callback(char* topic, byte* payload, unsigned int msg_length) {
Serial.print("Message arrived [");
Serial.print(topic);
Serial.print("] ");
for( int i = 0; i < msg_length; i++) {
Serial.print((char)payload[i]);
    }
Serial.println();

    // Switch on the LED if an 1 was received as first character
if ((char)payload[0] == '0') {
digitalWrite(OUTDOOR_LIGHT, LOW);   // Turn the LED off
    } else {
digitalWrite(OUTDOOR_LIGHT, HIGH);  // Turn the LED on
    }
}
```

In the `reconnect()` function, it will also subscribe to the `outdoor/light` topic from which it will get the messages and if the connection with the broker is lost it will try to connect to it every five seconds:

```
void reconnect() {
  // Loop until we're reconnected
while (!client.connected()) {
Serial.print("Attempting MQTT connection...");
    // Attempt to connect
if (client.connect("ESP8266Client"))
    {
Serial.println("connected");
```

```
client.subscribe("outdoor/light");
    } else {
Serial.print("failed, rc=");
Serial.print(client.state());
Serial.println(" try again in 5 seconds");
    // Wait 5 seconds before retrying
delay(5000);
    }
  }
}
```

The loop() function will publish the value of the GPIO 12, which is actually the state of the outdoor light:

```
void loop() {

if (!client.connected()) {
reconnect();
  }
client.loop();

long now = millis();
if (now - lastMsg> 2000) {
lastMsg = now;
    String light_state;

if(digitalRead(OUTDOOR_LIGHT) == HIGH)
light_state = "ON";
else
light_state = "OFF";


Serial.print("Publish message: ");
Serial.println(light_state);
client.publish("outdoor/light/status", light_state.c_str());
  }
}
```

In the Terminal window, you will see **ON** or **OFF** depending on the value of the last message transmitted on the `outdoor/light` topic. Please note the module is subscribing to the topic `outdoor/light` and is publishing the status of the GPIO on the `outdoor/light/status` topic:

```
catalin@plex:~$ mosquitto_sub -h 192.168.1.116 -t outdoor/light/status    WiFi connected
OFF                                                                        IP address:
OFF                                                                        192.168.1.142
OFF                                                                        Attempting MQTT connection...connected
OFF                                                                        Publish message: OFF
OFF                                                                        Publish message: OFF
OFF                                                                        Publish message: OFF
OFF                                                                        Publish message: OFF
OFF                                                                        Publish message: OFF
ON                                                                         Publish message: OFF
ON                                                                         Message arrived [outdoor/light] 1
ON                                                                         Publish message: ON
ON                                                                         Publish message: ON
OFF                                                                        Publish message: ON
OFF                                                                        Message arrived [outdoor/light] 0
OFF                                                                        Publish message: OFF
                                                                           Publish message: OFF
                                                  catalin@plex: ~          Publish message: OFF
                                                                           Publish message: OFF
File  Edit  Tabs  Help                                                     Message arrived [outdoor/light] 1
                                                                           Publish message: ON
catalin@plex:~$ mosquitto_pub -h 192.168.1.116 -t outdoor/light -m 1       Publish message: ON
catalin@plex:~$ mosquitto_pub -h 192.168.1.116 -t outdoor/light -m 0       Publish message: ON
catalin@plex:~$ mosquitto_pub -h 192.168.1.116 -t outdoor/light -m 1       Publish message: ON
catalin@plex:~$ mosquitto_pub -h 192.168.1.116 -t outdoor/light -m 0       Message arrived [outdoor/light] 0
catalin@plex:~$                                                            Publish message: OFF
catalin@plex:~$                                                            Publish message: OFF
catalin@plex:~$                                                            Publish message: OFF
catalin@plex:~$                                                            Publish message: OFF
catalin@plex:~$                                                            Publish message: OFF
catalin@plex:~$                                                            Publish message: OFF
```

Sending and receiving messages

Securing Mosquitto

If your Mosquitto MQTT broker is in the cloud it is a good idea to secure it at least with a user and password.

Mosquitto offers the `mosquitto_passwd` utility, which allows us to create a user and a password. You will be invited to enter a password and to confirm it:

```
sudo mosquito_passwd -c /etc/mosquito/passwd    joe
```

In the `/etc/mosquitto` directory a file named `passwd` will be created and in the file will be a user named `joe` and its encoded password as in the following screenshot:

```
catalin@plex:/etc/mosquitto$ more passwd
joe:$6$lKVIyEERoF0VwJ8n$N0qL+vAJkHkwRXX9Y16fB2XoHJOJm23wa64DnmBVf+M/3FOYLvWK5BblWaMwZ1CleQkco+J0IE6dGL4dlDRWuQ==
```

Now let's add the `passwd` file into the `mosquitto.conf`. Use your favorite text editor and change the `file /etc/mosquitto.conf` to instruct Mosquitto to read and use the `passwd` file.

The content of the file will be:

```
# Place your local configuration in /etc/mosquitto/conf.d/
#
# A full description of the configuration file is at
# /usr/share/doc/mosquitto/examples/mosquitto.conf.example

pid_file /var/run/mosquitto.pid

persistence true
persistence_location /var/lib/mosquitto/

log_dest file /var/log/mosquitto/mosquitto.log

allow_anonymous false
password_file /etc/mosquitto/passwd

include_dir /etc/mosquitto/conf.d
```

Password file location

- `allow_anonymous`: It is a boolean value that determines whether clients that connects without providing a username are allowed to connect. If set to `false` then another means a connection should be created to control authenticated client access.
- `password_file`: Sets the path to a password file. If defined, the contents of the file are used to control client access to the broker. If `allow_anonymous` is set to `false`, only users defined in this file will be able to connect.

After stopping and restarting the Mosquitto service using the commands:

```
sudo service mosquitto stop && sudo service mosquitto start
```

If a terminal window will try to connect as you did before, we will receive an error message like in the following screenshot:

```
catalin@plex:/etc/mosquitto$ mosquitto_sub -t living/temperature
Connection Refused: not authorised.
Connection Refused: not authorised.
Connection Refused: not authorised.
Connection Refused: not authorised.
Connection Refused: not authorised.
```

But subscribing and publishing with the user and the password created before will work. For subscribing the command is:

```
sudo mosquitto_sub -t living/temperature -u joe -P joe1234
```

And for publishing:

```
sudo mosquitto_pub -t living/temperature -u joe -P joe1234 -m {"t":24.7}
```

 Make sure you use capital a P for the password and not, p which is for port.

You will get the following result:

```
catalin@plex:/etc/mosquitto$ mosquitto_sub -t living/temperature -u joe -P joe1234

{t:24.7}
{t:24.7}
{t:24.7}
{t:24.7}
{t:24.7}
```

Providing username and password

Now let's use ESP8266 to send the username and password to the broker:

```
#include <ESP8266WiFi.h>
#include <PubSubClient.h>
```

Update these with values suitable for your network:

```
const char* wifi_network = "WiFi 176-58";
const char* password = "P6etRUzaRa";
const char* mqtt_serv_address = "192.168.1.116";
const char* mqtt_user = "joe";
const char* mqtt_passwd = "joe1234";
const int   mqtt_port_number = 1883;
#define OUTDOOR_LIGHT  12
```

The `mqtt_user` will keep the value of the username and the `mqtt_passwd` will keep the user's password. We will use them in the connect method and pass them to the server:

```
WiFiClient  espClient;
PubSubClient    client(espClient);
long  lastMsg = 0;

void setup() {
pinMode(OUTDOOR_LIGHT, OUTPUT);       // Initialize the BUILTIN_LED pin as an
output
Serial.begin(115200);
setup_wifi();
client.setServer(mqtt_serv_address, mqtt_port_number);
client.setCallback(callback);
}

void setup_wifi() {

delay(10);
  // We start by connecting to a WiFi network
Serial.println();
Serial.print("Connecting to ");
Serial.println(wifi_network);

WiFi.begin(ssid, password);

while (WiFi.status() != WL_CONNECTED) {
WiFi.begin(wifi_network, password);

Serial.print(".");
delay(5000);
  }

Serial.println("");
Serial.println("WiFi connected");
Serial.println("IP address: ");
Serial.println(WiFi.localIP());
}


void callback(char* topic, byte* payload, unsigned int msg_length) {
Serial.print("Message arrived [");
Serial.print(topic);
Serial.print("] ");
for (int i = 0; i< msg_length; i++) {
Serial.print((char)payload[i]);
  }
Serial.println();
```

```
    // Switch on the LED if an 1 was received as first character
if ((char)payload[0] == '0') {
digitalWrite(OUTDOOR_LIGHT, LOW);    // Turn the LED off
    } else {
digitalWrite(OUTDOOR_LIGHT, HIGH);   // Turn the LED on
    }
}

void reconnect() {
  // Loop until we're reconnected
while (!client.connected()) {
Serial.print("Attempting MQTT connection...");
```

Attempt to connect to the MQTT Mosquitto broker using the username and the password from `mqtt_user` and `mqtt_passwd`:

```
if (client.connect("ESP8266Client", mqtt_user, mqtt_passwd))
{
  Serial.println("connected");
  client.subscribe("outdoor/light");
} else {
  Serial.print("failed, rc=");
  Serial.print(client.state());
  Serial.println(" try again in 5 seconds");
  // Wait 5 seconds before retrying
  delay(5000);
  }
 }
}

void loop() {

if (!client.connected()) {
    reconnect();
}
client.loop();

long now = millis();
if (now - lastMsg> 2000) {
    lastMsg = now;
    String light_state;

    if(digitalRead(OUTDOOR_LIGHT) == HIGH)
       light_state = "ON";
    else
       light_state = "OFF";
```

```
        Serial.print("Publish message: ");
        Serial.println(light_state);
        client.publish("outdoor/light/status", light_state.c_str());
    }
}
```

Publishing a message with the payload 1 will trigger the GPIO 12 and turn on the connected LED in a secure way. The ON OFF messages are the state of the GPIO where on ON will have 3V3 and on OFF 0V:

```
catalin@plex:/etc/mosquitto$ mosquitto_sub -t outdoor/light/status -u joe -P joe1234
OFF
OFF
OFF
ON
ON
ON
ON
OFF
OFF
OFF
```

Receiving ON/OFF messages

Now, sending this message from any place in the world will turn on and off any appliance from your house, if instead of the LED we will add a relay board:

```
Until now small messages were used, by default the maximum size allowed by
the PubSubClient is 128 bytes. If your messages are bigger than 128 bytes,
go to the PubSubClient.h file and change the value for
MQTT_MAX_PACKET_SIZE.
```

Summary

Using an MQTT server such as Mosquitto is very important because it allows you to communicate machine to machine M2M and you can start to automate many tasks from turning on the lights in the house if is a cloudy day to automatically controling your house's climate.

3
Building a Home Thermostat with the ESP8266

In this chapter, we will build a home thermostat with ESP8266. The thermostat will have the following functions:

- It will read the temperature from a DHT22 temperature sensor
- It will compare the temperature with the desired one; if it is above it, it will trigger a relay OFF and if it is below, it will trigger the relay ON

But first, let's discuss how we can save data in the ESP8266 and retrieve it. Let's make use of SPIFFS.

SPIFFS

SPI Flash File System (SPIFFS) is a filesystem created for small embedded systems. SPIFFS has many advantages since it allows you to create files and simulate directories.

The following are the features of SPIFFS:

- Designed for low RAM use on microcontrollers
- Uses statically sized RAM buffers
- Posix-like api: open, close, read, write, seek, stat, and so on
- It can run on any NOR flash, not only the SPI flash. Multiple SPIFFS configurations can run on the same target - and even on the same SPI flash device

- Implements static wear levelling
- Built-in filesystem consistency checks
- Highly configurable and can be adapted for a variety of flash types

I highly encourage you to use SPIFFS in your designs to store data in NOR flash since it is very easy to read and write data, is like a *nix filesystem.

Filesystem size depends on the flash chip size. Depending on the board that is selected in the IDE, you can select different sizes for SPIFFS. For example, in case if you have selected the NodeMcu v1.0 as Board type, there are two dimensions for the SPIFFS, one of 1M and 3M as shown in the following screenshot:

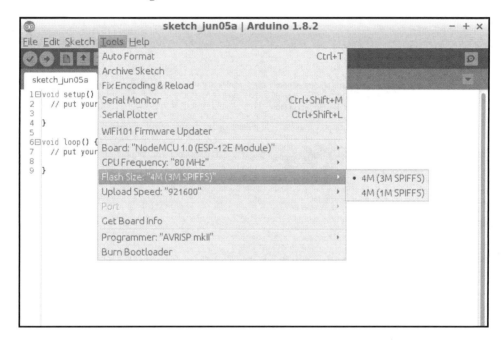

Flash size for NodeMcu

Even though the filesystem is stored on the same flash chip as the application program, flashing a new sketch will not modify the filesystem contents. This allows us to use the filesystem to store data, configuration files, or content for web servers.

Let's now see what functions are available to manipulate files. First of all they have access to the SPIFFS function and the FS.h file need to be included in the sketch:

```
#include "FS.h"
```

After this inclusion we have access to three objects: SPIFFS, File, and Dir. We will learn about these objects in detail in the following sections.

SPIFFS objects

Let's look at few SPIFFS objects:

- `begin` : Mounts the filesystem. Needs to be called first and returns `true` for success or `false` otherwise:

```
if(SPIFFS.begin())
{
  Serial.println(F("File systestem mounted.")); //use F function to
store the string in flash and not in RAM memory. This save a lot of
RAM memory
}
else
{
  Serial.println(F("Mounting file system failed."));
}
```

- `info`: Returns information about the entire filesystem, information that is stored in the `FSInfo` structure. The `FSInfo` structure has the following members:

```
struct FSInfo {
    size_t totalBytes;
    size_t usedBytes;
    size_t blockSize;
    size_t pageSize;
    size_t maxOpenFiles;
    size_t maxPathLength;
};
```

Declaring the `fs_info` and populating it with the `info` function will allow us to access information about the filesystem:

```
FSInfo fs_info;
SPIFFS.info(fs_info);
Serial.print("Used bytes: ");
Serial.println(fs_info.usedBytes);
```

- exists: `SPIFFS.exists(path)` returns `true` or `false` if the specified path (file) exists in the filesystem:

```
if(SPIFFS.exist("/config.json"))
    Serial.println(F("File config.json exists."));
```

The path must be an absolute path and starting with a slash.

- format: Formats the entire filesystem and returns `true` or `false`. Format can be called before or after the `begin` function and it takes some tens of seconds to complete depending on your filesystem size:

```
SPIFFS.format();
```

- open: This function returns a `File` object and takes as parameters the absolute path for the file and the mode for opening the file. Returns `true` for success or `false` otherwise:

```
SPIFFS.open(path, mode);

File config_file = SPIFFS.open("/config.json", "w");
if (!config_file) {
    Serial.println(F("failed opening config.json file."));
}
```

In the preceding code the selected mode for opening the file was w (write). The same modes as the ANSI C function `fopen` can be used:

r   Open text file for reading. The stream is positioned at the beginning of the file.

r+ Open for reading and writing. The stream is positioned at the beginning of the file.

w   Truncate file to zero length or create a text file for writing. The stream is positioned at the beginning of the file.

w+ Open for reading and writing. The file is created if it does not exist; otherwise it is truncated. The stream is positioned at the beginning of the file.

a   Open for appending (writing at end of file). The file is created if it does not exist. The stream is positioned at the end of the file.

a+ Open for reading and appending (writing at end of file). The file is created if it does not exist. The initial file position for reading is at the beginning of the file, but output is always appended to the end of the file.

- remove: Remove the file from the filesystem. It takes as a parameter the absolute path and returns `true` for success or `false` otherwise:

```
if(SPIFFS.remove("/config.json"))
    Serial.println(F("File config.json was removed"));
```

- rename: Renames the file. Takes two parameters, absolute paths for current name and new name. Returns `true` if successful or `false` otherwise:

```
If( SPIFFS.rename("/old_file_name.json","/new_file_name.json")
    Serial.println(F("File renamed."));
```

Directory object

In case you need to iterate on all the files from a directory you can use the **Dir** (Directory) object. There are three methods available to iterate `next()`, get the name of the next file file `Name()` and to open the directory `openDir(mode)`:

 SPIFFS doesn't support directories. In fact it produces a flat structure. Creating a file with path `/data/log.txt` will create a file called `/data/log.txt` instead of `log.txt` under the directory data.

```
Dir dir = SPIFFS.openDir("/data");
while (dir.next()) {
    Serial.print(dir.fileName());
    File f = dir.openFile("r");
    Serial.println(f.size());
}
```

From the preceding code we learn that:

- mode from `openDir` can have the same values as the `open` function from the `SPIFFS` object
- `dir.next()` returns true if there are files in the data directory and must be called before the `fileName()` and `openFile(mode)` functions

File object

There are two functions that return a `File` object, `SPIFFS.open` and `dir.OpenFile` and this `File` object allows us to read bytes, peek into file, and get the current position in file, get the name of the file or its size. The following are the various functions used by the File object:

- `close`: Close the file. No other operations should be performed on the `File` object after the `close()` function was called:

  ```
  file_name.close();
  ```

- `name`: Returns the name of the current file:

  ```
  String name = my_file.name();
  ```

- `position`: Returns the current position in the file in bytes. You can use it if you are storing same size data and iterare in the file.

- `seek`: Allows you to move into a file. It take two parameters; one is the offset in the file and the other is the mode. Returns `true` for success and `false` otherwise:

  ```
  my_file.seek(offset, mode);
  ```

- Parameter `mode` can have the same values as it has in the `fseek()` C function:

    If `mode` is `SeekSet`, the position is set to offset bytes from the beginning

    If `mode` is `SeekCur`, the current position is moved by offset bytes

    If `mode` is `SeekEnd`, the position is set to offset bytes from the end of the file

- `size`: Get the current file size in bytes:

  ```
  Serial.println(my_file.size());
  ```

As an example let's create a file, write something in it, and read what was written; if the GPIO 4 is put to GND, it will format the flash.

If you remember, `FS.h` needs to be included to have access to the SPIFFS object:

```
#include "FS.h"
```

Set the `interruptPin` to value 4, and instantiate the `interruptCounter` to zero:

```
const byte interruptPin = 4;
volatile byte interruptCounter = 0;
```

This function will be called if the GPIO is put to GND. In it it will increment the `interruptCounter` and will be verifying its value in the `loop()` function. Try not to allocate memory at interrupt level; this is a recipe for disaster:

```
void handleInterrupt() {
  interruptCounter++;
}
```

In `setup()`, we will set the GPIO 4 as input pin and use the `attacheInterrupt` function for `FALLING` (VCC to GND) to trigger the `handleInterrupt` function. Next we open the `my_file.txt` and write a message in it. After the file is closed, it will be opened again, but now it is in read mode and it will read its content:

```
void setup() {
  Serial.begin(115200); delay(10);
  //GPIO 4 format SPIFFS
  pinMode(interruptPin, INPUT_PULLUP);
  attachInterrupt(digitalPinToInterrupt(interruptPin), handleInterrupt,
FALLING);

  if(SPIFFS.begin())
  {
    Serial.println(F("File system was mounted."));
    // open file for writing
    File my_file = SPIFFS.open("/my_file.txt", "w+");
    if (!my_file) {
      Serial.println("file open failed");
    }
    Serial.println(F("Writing to SPIFFS "));
    //print something to my_file.txt
    my_file.println("SPIFFS is cool!");
    //close now the file
    my_file.close();

    // open file for reading. Now I can use other File object
    File f = SPIFFS.open("/my_file.txt", "r");
    if (!f)
    {
      Serial.println(F("Failed to open my_file.txt"));
    }
    //now read the file content
    String s=f.readStringUntil('\n');
```

```
    Serial.println(s);
    //closing the file now
    f.close();
  }
  else
  {
    Serial.println(F("Failed to mount SPIFFS. Restart"));
    ESP.restart();
  }
}
```

In the loop file we check for the `intrruptCounter` value and if it is greater than zero it will format the filesystem and restart the ESP:

```
void loop()
{
  if(interruptCounter>0)
  {
    interruptCounter--;
    Serial.println(F("Formating the file system... Please wait!"));
    SPIFFS.format();
    Serial.println(F("Done formating the file system."));
    ESP.restart();
  }
}
```

The Serial output will show what was read from the file, also the formating messages and the new restart after that, as seen in the following screenshot:

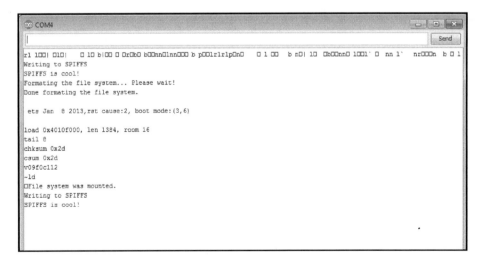

Output for write, read, and format

Now that you have managed to understand the SPIFFS I am sure that you will use it in all your projects since it is a very handy way to keep configuration data or to store all kinds of information such as readings from sensors, especially if you are running on batteries. You can store all the readings in a file in JSON format and once a day connect to Wi-Fi, read the file, and send all the data at once.

After this long but useful introduction, let's go back to our project, a thermostat using the ESP8266. To complete this, besides the ESP8266 we need:

- Temperature sensor
- Relay board

Temperature sensor

There are a lot of temperature sensors that can be used, but for this project we will use a very common one, the DTH22. It can measure temperature and humidity.

The following are the DHT22 characteristics:

- Low cost
- 3 to 5V power and I/O
- 5mA max current used during conversion (while requesting data)
- Good for 0-100% humidity readings with 2-5% accuracy
- Good for -40 to 125°C temperature readings ±0.5°C accuracy
- No more than 0.5 Hz sampling rate (once every two seconds)
- Body size 15.1mm x 25mm x 7.7mm
- 4 pins with 0.1" spacing

DHT22 can be found as a separate sensor or as a breakout. It is preferrable to buy the breakout version since it has also the pull-up 4k7 resistor and a capacitor. If you prefer the sensor alone this is the pinout:

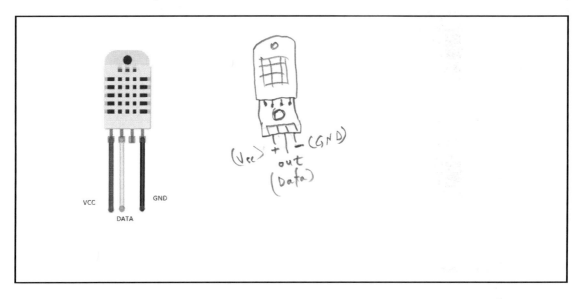

DHT22 pinout

Here:

- **VCC**: can be between 3V3 and 5V
- **GND**: is the ground
- **DATA**: is the data pin

Don't forget to add a 4K7 pull-up resistor between the DATA and VCC pin. For the connection with a gas furnance or other heating element, a relay will be added on the GPIO 12. Make sure that you have a good power supply since the relay will absorb some energy.

In this case, our setup will be:

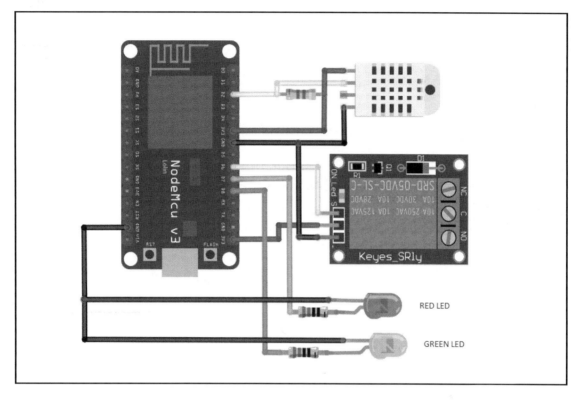

Final circuit for thermostat

Two LEDs were added, one **RED LED** to show that heating is in progress and one **GREEN LED** to show that the system has power. The green LED will light only when the red one is not on.

On the relay board, the connection between the **C (common)** and **NO (normal open)** exists only when the GPIO 12 is HIGH, and heating is in progress.

Be careful with the 220V electricity and make sure we choose a relay that can hold your consumed power.

Basically the thermostat will measure temperature and if it is above the desired one it will turn the relay OFF and if it is below it will turn the relay ON to start heating.

If we do our logic like that the thermostat will turn the relay ON and OFF very often so we need to add an offset (delta) between the start and stop of heating. On commercial thermostats this offset can be programmed (in 0.1ºC steps up to 1ºC) or can be fixed like 0.5ºC.

In our system the offset will be set to 0.4ºC. This means that, if our desired temperature is 22.0ºC, the heater will start at 21.6ºC and will stop at 22.4ºC.

To set up the desired temperature on our thermostat we will send a MQTT message to the topic `thermostat/set` with the content of desired temperature (for instance 23.2); the system will save the value in a file with the help of SPIFFS and will compare it with the current temperature read from the DHT22 sensor. In the event of power failure, the desired temperature will be read from the configuration file so it is not lost.

When the thermostat is powered on for the first time the desired temperature is hardcoded to 22ºC. Periodically the thermostat will publish on the `thermostat/get` the currrent temperature as it is sensed by the DHT22.

In order to use the DHT22 sensor you will need some libraries for it. Install the **Adafruit Unified Sensor** and after that the **DHT sensor library** following the same procedure like in the `Chapter 1`, *Getting Started with the ESP8266*.

For the `Adafruit Unified Sensor` search in the **Library Manager** for `Adafruit Unified Sensor`:

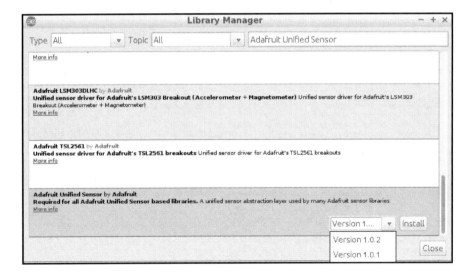

For the `DHT22` library search in the Library Manager for `DHT22`:

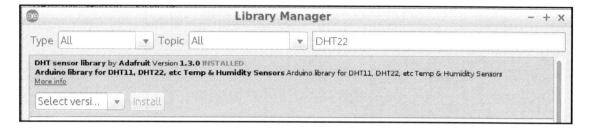

After installing both libraries now we have all the necessary headers are as follows:

```
#include <FS.h>
#include <ESP8266WiFi.h>
#include <PubSubClient.h>
#include <DHT.h>
```

Constants that will be used later in our code are as follows. Make sure that you have the correct values:

```
const char* ssid = "YOUR_WIFI_SSID";
const char* password = "YOUR_WIFI_PASSWORD";
const char* mqtt_server = "YOUR_MQTT_SERVER";
const char* mqtt_user = "YOUR_MQTT_USER";
const char* mqtt_passwd = "YOUR_MQTT_PASSWORD";
const int mqtt_port = 1883; //YOUR_MQTT_PORT
```

The relay module is connected to the GPIO 12, DHT22 to pin 4, and LEDs to GPIO 13 and GPIO 15 are as follows:

```
#define RELAY_PIN   12
#define DHTTYPE DHT22
#define DHTPIN   4
#define GREEN_LED 15
#define RED_LED 13
```

Our global objects and default values for offset and desired temperature:

```
WiFiClient espClient;
PubSubClient client(espClient);
DHT dht(DHTPIN, DHTTYPE, 11);
long lastMsg = 0;
float offset_temp = 0.4;
float desired_temp = 22.0;
float humidity, temp_f;  // Values read from sensor
```

not needed w/ new library?

`gettemperature()` is getting the temperature and humidity from the DHT22 sensor and saves them into the global variables `humidity` and `temp_f`. If you need temperatures in Fahrenheit, call the `dht.readTemperature()` function with true as a parameter such as `dht.readTemperature(true);`:

```
void gettemperature()
{
  int runs=0;
  do {
        temp_f = dht.readTemperature(false);
        humidity = dht.readHumidity();

        if(runs > 0)
        {
            Serial.println("##Failed to read from DHT sensor! ###");
        }
//        Serial.println(String(temp_f ).c_str());
//        Serial.println(String(humidity ).c_str());
        runs++;
    }
    while(isnan(temp_f) && isnan(humidity));
}
```

The set-up part is where the pins for relay and LEDs are set as OUTPUT and the green LED is on as the default on power start, as follows:

```
void setup() {
  pinMode(RELAY_PIN, OUTPUT);
  pinMode(GREEN_LED, OUTPUT);
  pinMode(RED_LED, OUTPUT);
  digitalWrite(RELAY_PIN, LOW);
  digitalWrite(GREEN_LED, HIGH);
  digitalWrite(RED_LED, LOW);

  Serial.begin(115200);
  setup_wifi();
  client.setServer(mqtt_server, mqtt_port);
  client.setCallback(callback);

  if(SPIFFS.begin())
  {
    Serial.println(F("File system was mounted."));
    //check to see if we have a desired temperature other then default one
    File f = SPIFFS.open("/config_temp.txt", "r");
    if (!f)
    {
      //now read the file content
```

```
       String s=f.readStringUntil('\n');
       Serial.println(s);
       desired_temp = s.toFloat();
       //closing the file now
       f.close();
     }
     else
       Serial.println(F("Failed to open my_file.txt"));
   }
 }
```

Connect to the Wi-Fi network with the provided credentials, as follows:

```
void setup_wifi() {

  delay(10);
  // We start by connecting to a WiFi network
  Serial.println();
  Serial.print(F("Connecting to "));
  Serial.println(ssid);

  WiFi.begin(ssid, password);

  while (WiFi.status() != WL_CONNECTED)
  {
    WiFi.begin(ssid, password);

    Serial.print(".");
    delay(5000);
  }
  Serial.println(F("WiFi connected"));
  Serial.println(F("IP address: "));
  Serial.println(WiFi.localIP());
}
```

The following is the `callback` function that is triggered when a new MQTT message is received on the subscribed topic `thermostart/set`:

```
void callback(char* topic, byte* payload, unsigned int length)
{
  Serial.print(F("Message arrived ["));
  Serial.print(topic);
  Serial.print(F("] "));

  for (int i = 0; i < length; i++) {
    Serial.print((char)payload[i]);
  }
  Serial.println();
```

```
char rxj[20];
int i;
for(i=0;i<length;i++)
{
   rxj[i] = payload[i];
}

File my_file = SPIFFS.open("/config_temp.txt", "w+");
if (!my_file) {
    Serial.println("file open failed");
}
Serial.println(F("Writing to config_temp.txt "));
//print something to my_file.txt
my_file.println(String(rxj).c_str());
//close now the file
my_file.close();
desired_temp = String(rxj).toFloat();
}
```

Reconnect to the MQTT server in case some keep alive frames are lost, as shown in the following code:

```
void reconnect() {
  // Loop until we're reconnected
  while (!client.connected()) {
    Serial.print(F("Attempting MQTT connection..."));
    if (client.connect("ESP8266Client", mqtt_user, mqtt_passwd))
    {
      Serial.println(F("connected"));
      client.subscribe("thermostat/set");
    } else {
      Serial.print(F("failed, rc="));
      Serial.print(client.state());
      Serial.println(F(" try again in 5 seconds"));
      // Wait 5 seconds before retrying
      delay(5000);
    }
  }
}
```

The loop function is where our logic for triggering the relay and LEDs ON or OFF exists. Every two seconds it reads the temperature and checks it with our desired one, as follows:

```
void loop()
{

  gettemperature();
  if (!client.connected()) {
```

```
    reconnect();
  }
  client.loop();

  long now = millis();
  if (now - lastMsg > 2000) {
    lastMsg = now;

    if((float)desired_temp - offset_temp >= (float)temp_f)
    {
      //Serial.println(F("Start heating..."));
      digitalWrite(RELAY_PIN, HIGH);
      digitalWrite(GREEN_LED, LOW);
      digitalWrite(RED_LED, HIGH);
    }
    else if((float)desired_temp + offset_temp <= (float)temp_f)
    {
      //Serial.println(F("Stop heating..."));
      digitalWrite(RELAY_PIN, LOW);
      digitalWrite(GREEN_LED, HIGH);
      digitalWrite(RED_LED, LOW);
    }
    client.publish("thermostat/get", String(temp_f).c_str());
  }
}
```

To set up the temperature you can use a local console of your MQTT broker like we did in
Chapter 2, *Building and Configuring Your Own MQTT Server*:

```
mosquitto_pub -t "thermostat/set" -m 28.2 -p 1883 -h YOUR_MQTT_SERVE_IP -u
YOUR_MQTT_USER -P YOUR_MQTT_PASSWORD
```

And if you subscribe to the thermostat/get topic you will get the current temperature in
your room every two seconds, as shown in the following screenshot:

Room temperature received from MQTT broker

For Android phones there is an application called MyMQTT and if your broker is accessible from the Internet, you can set up your desired temperature when you are not at home; you can see also the current temperature in your house.

The main menu for this MyMQTT application is as follows:

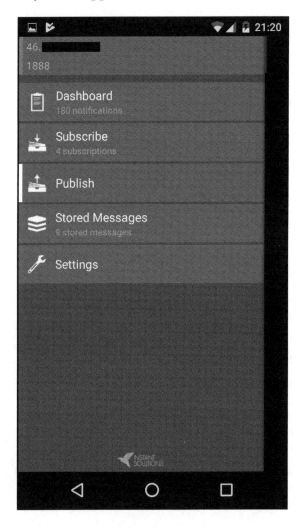

MyMQTT main screen

In the **Settings** menu, set up the MQTT broker IP address, the MQTT port used, and the user and password.

After saving the configuration, the application will connect to your broker. To see the messages from your broker you can subscribe to the # topic; in this case you will see all the messages received by the broker (as shown in the following screenshot), or to the `thermostart/get` to receive just the temperature from your home:

Receive the temperature from thermostat

If you are away you can remotely set the thermostat by publishing a message with the desired temperature to your home thermostat on the topic `thermostat/set`, as shown in the following screenshot:

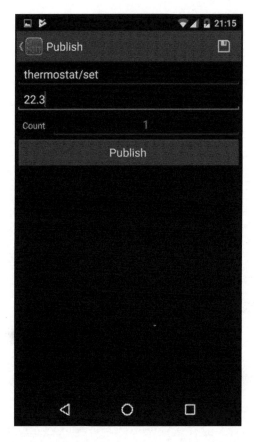

Publish desired temperature to control your thermostat

This basic functional thermostat system taught you how to use SPIFFS to store files and values, to send and receive values from MQTT brokers, and store them in a file to read temperature and humidity from a sensor. As an exercise, you can improve the thermostat with the following functionalities:

- Publish the humidity as well
- Save the config file as an JSON file

- Add a chronothermostat functionality to heat your home just between programmed hours
- Add a window open functionality to stop heating the house if the temperature drops very quickly
- Publish the temperature, humidity, and desired temperature as a JSON message over MQTT
- Use reverse logic to cool your house in the hot summers.

Summary

In this chapter, you learned how to save your data to the SPIFFS and how to build and control a thermostat. So far, the credentials for the Wi-Fi have been hard coded in the code; in the next chapter we will learn how to use the `WiFiManager` library to expose an Access Point. Get the Wi-Fi credentials along with other data and save them to the flash, making use of SPIFFS.

Control Appliances from the ESP8266

If you want to create an IoT module as a commercial product and sell it, you will need to let the user configure the Wi-Fi credentials themselves as long as the MQTT server, port, username and password that will be used by user. All the extra information needs to be stored on the SPIFFS filesystem so when the module will start will be used to connect to Wi-Fi and to connect to the MQTT server.

In the first part of this chapter, we will discuss how to build a web server to get Wi-Fi network credentials with the help of the `WiFiManager` library, save them to the SPIFFS file, and in the second part, we will build a module that allows you to control a TV using infra-red.

By the end of this chapter, you will have gained the knowledge to start your first commercial IoT product.

Using the WiFiManager library

Until now the SSID and password for connecting the ESP8266 to the Wi-Fi network have been hardcoded in the sketch using these lines:

```
const char* ssid = "YOUR_WIFI_SSID";
const char* password = "YOUR_WIFI_PASSWORD";
```

To stop using the hardcoded values we need to first start the ESP8266 in AP mode and expose the user as a web interface served by an embedded web server hosted inside the ESP8266.

We will learn how to use the WiFiManager library to expose a configuration web page; we will take the data and save it to a SPIFFS like we did in the previous chapter and use it to start our module in station mode and connect to an MQTT server.

If you didn't install the WiFiManager library in Chapter 1, *Getting Started with the ESP8266* you can do it now, going to **Sketch** | **Include Library** | **Manage libraries** and search for wifimanager, as seen in the following screenshot:

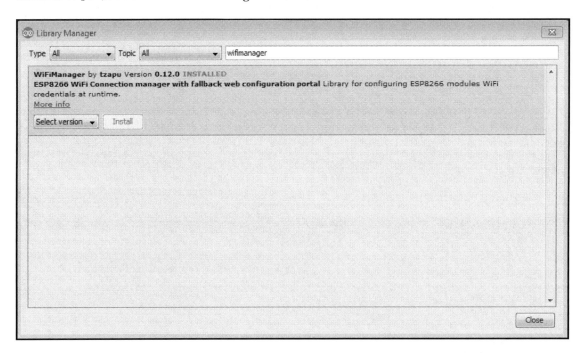

Installing the WiFiManager library

After the installation of the library, let's see how you can use it to set the Wi-Fi network and Wi-Fi password.

Use the following code to see how it looks and how to use the WiFiManager:

```
#include "FS.h"
#include <ESP8266WiFi.h>
#include <DNSServer.h>
#include <ESP8266WebServer.h>
#include <WiFiManager.h>
```

In case you need to clear the previously saved values in the SPIFFS you can set `init_esp` to `true` to clean the previously stored Wi-Fi credentials and to format the SPIFFS. This can be the case when you want to move the ESP8266 module to a different WiFi network. After you flash the code the `setup()` function will format the SPIFFS. Change then the value back to false so you will not format the flash every time when the ESP8266 is starting:

```
boolean init_esp = false;
void setup()
{
  Serial.begin(115200); delay(10);

  if(init_esp)
  {
    SPIFFS.format();
    WiFi.disconnect();
  }
```

Instantiate the `wifiManager` object. This will start the ESP in the access Point mode and a captive portal that will redirect you to a configuration web page:

```
WiFiManager wifiManager;
```

Set the expiration timeout to 240 seconds:

```
wifiManager.setConfigPortalTimeout(240);
if (!wifiManager.autoConnect("ESP_AP", "changeit"))
{
  Serial.println(F("Failed to connect. Reset and try again..."));
  delay(3000);
  //reset and try again
  ESP.reset();
  delay(5000);
}
```

At this point we are connected now to the Wi-Fi network, after we selected the Wi-Fi network and password from a web browser:

```
//if you get here you have connected to the WiFi
Serial.println(F("Connected to Wifi."));
Serial.print(F("My IP: "));
Serial.println(WiFi.localIP());
}

void loop() {
  //add your code for loop()
}
```

After you compile and flash the ESP8266 with this code, take your phone and look for surrounding Wi-Fi networks. You will see a network named `ESP_AP`. Connect to it, enter the password `changeit`, and click on **Sign in to network**. If you don't see this message, go to your web browser and try to access any link or enter `192.168.4.1` in the address bar. You will be redirected to this page:

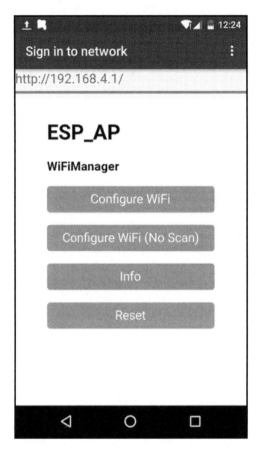

WiFiManager main screen

In this page you will see the access point name that was defined, **ESP_AP** and four buttons, which are explained in the following list:

- **Configure WiFi**: Scan surrounding Wi-Fi networks around and it will show you a list of them together with their signal power. If you have multiple Wi-Fi networks you can choose the one with the most power, as shown in the following screenshot:

Configure with scan

- **Configure WiFi (No Scan)**: If your Wi-Fi network has a hidden SSID or your Wi-Fi network is not online you can enter the name of the network and the password, skipping the scanning feature, as seen in the following screenshot:

Configure without scanning

- **Info**: As shown in the following screenshot, this page will read the Chip Id, MAC address for the access point or Station Mode of the ESP8266, and the flash details such as flash size and flash Id:

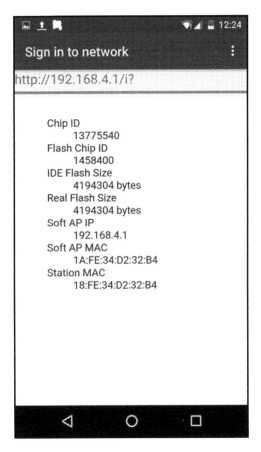

Information about ESP and flash

- **Reset**: Pressing the **Reset** button will reset the ESP8266 chip. In the Serial console from the Arduino IDE after the ESP is started, you will see some debug information about `WiFiManager`. If you want more information, then add the following line into your sketch:

```
wifiManager.setDebugOutput(false);
```

- After the line:

```
WiFiManager wifiManager;
```

- After the Wi-Fi network selected and the password introduced, the output in the serial console will show that the ESP is connected to the Wi-Fi; it will and also will show the IP address assigned by your router, as shown in the following screenshot:

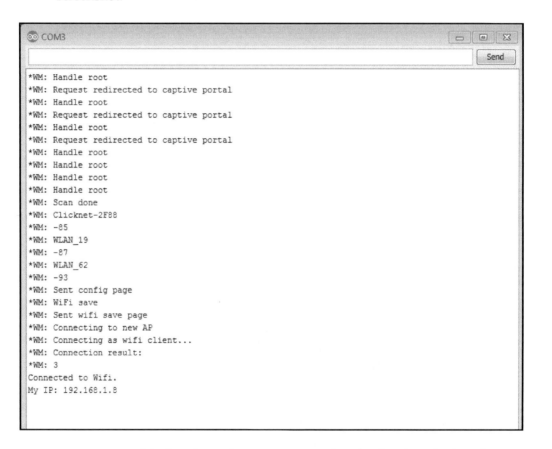

 You can add a hardware button connected to the GPIO and when the button is pressed the Wi-Fi credentials can be deleted, the flash can be formatted or some files from it can be deleted; thus, so you are not forced to flash the sketch if you want to change the Wi-Fi network, or the Wi-Fi password.

Adding parameters to the WiFiManager setup page and saving them into the file

So far, the only parameters saved from the WiFiManager page were the SSID and password for your network. Let's add other parameters such as the MQTT server, port, user, password and topic and save them to a configuration file located in the SPIFFS:

```
#include <FS.h>
#include <ESP8266WiFi.h>
#include <PubSubClient.h>
#include <DNSServer.h>
#include <ESP8266WebServer.h>
#include <WiFiManager.h>
#include <ArduinoJson.h>
```

Define the CLIENT_ID that will be used to connect to the MQTT broker later:

```
#define CLIENT_ID           "ESP_%06X"
```

Define your default values here; if there are different values in config.json, they are overwritten:

```
char mqtt_server[40];
char mqtt_port[6] = "1883";
char mqtt_user[32];
char mqtt_pass[32];
char mqtt_topic[64];

char dev_name[50];
```

Set to true if you want to initialize the ESP again:

```
boolean clean_g = false;

WiFiClient espClient;
PubSubClient client(espClient);
```

This function will be triggered when the ESP8266 receives a message from the MQTT broker:

```
void mqtt_callback(char* topic, byte* payload, unsigned int length) {
  char rxj[512];
  for (int i = 0; i < length; i++) {
    rxj[i] = payload[i];
  }
  Serial.println(rxj);
}

//flag for saving data
bool saveConfig = false;

//callback notifying us of the need to save config
void saveConfigToFileFn () {
  Serial.println("Should save config");
  saveConfig = true;
}
```

This `setup` function is doing all the work; starting the `WiFiManager`, saving the entered data into the `config.json` file on the SPIFFS, reading the content of the file every time the ESP8266 starts and giving you access to all the saved data:

```
void setup() {
  // put your setup code here, to run once:
  Serial.begin(115200); delay(10);
  sprintf(dev_name, CLIENT_ID, ESP.getChipId());

  if(clean_g)
  {
    Serial.println(F("\n\nWait...I am formatting  the FLASH !!!"));
    SPIFFS.format();
    Serial.println(F("Done!"));
    WiFi.disconnect(true);
  }
```

If the `config.json` file exists, read its content, which is JSON formatted, and set the `mqtt` variables to their corresponding values:

```
  if (SPIFFS.begin()) {
    Serial.println("mounted file system");
    if (SPIFFS.exists("/config.json")) {
      //file exists, reading and loading
      Serial.println("reading config file");
      File configFile = SPIFFS.open("/config.json", "r");
      if (configFile) {
        Serial.println("opened config file");
```

```
      size_t size = configFile.size();
      // Allocate a buffer to store contents of the file.
      std::unique_ptr<char[]> buf(new char[size]);

      configFile.readBytes(buf.get(), size);
      DynamicJsonBuffer jsonBuffer;
      JsonObject& json = jsonBuffer.parseObject(buf.get());
      json.printTo(Serial);
      if (json.success()) {
        Serial.println("\nparsed json");

        strcpy(mqtt_server, json["mqtt_server"]);
        strcpy(mqtt_port, json["mqtt_port"]);
        strcpy(mqtt_user, json["mqtt_user"]);
        strcpy(mqtt_pass, json["mqtt_pass"]);
        strcpy(mqtt_topic, json["mqtt_topic"]);

      } else {
        Serial.println("failed to load json config");
      }
    }
  }
} else {
  Serial.println("failed to mount FS");
}
```

Add custom parameters to the `WiFiManager` so they're available when the user wants to set them through the web interface:

```
WiFiManagerParameter custom_mqtt_server("server", "mqtt server",
mqtt_server, 40);
  WiFiManagerParameter custom_mqtt_port("port", "mqtt port", mqtt_port, 5);
  WiFiManagerParameter custom_mqtt_user("user", "mqtt user", mqtt_user,
32);
  WiFiManagerParameter custom_mqtt_pass("pass", "mqtt pass", mqtt_pass,
32);
  WiFiManagerParameter custom_mqtt_topic("topic", "mqtt topic", mqtt_topic,
64);

WiFiManager wifiManager;

wifiManager.setSaveConfigCallback(saveConfigToFileFn);

wifiManager.addParameter(&custom_mqtt_server);
wifiManager.addParameter(&custom_mqtt_port);
wifiManager.addParameter(&custom_mqtt_user);
wifiManager.addParameter(&custom_mqtt_pass);
wifiManager.addParameter(&custom_mqtt_topic);
```

Start the WiFiManager Access Point with the name ESP_AP.

```
if (!wifiManager.autoConnect("ESP_AP"))
{
  Serial.println(F("failed to connect and hit timeout"));
  delay(3000);
  //reset and try again, or maybe put it to deep sleep
  ESP.reset();
  delay(5000);
}

Serial.println(F("WiFi is connected now..."));
```

Read the updated parameters from the web page:

```
strcpy(mqtt_server, custom_mqtt_server.getValue());
strcpy(mqtt_port, custom_mqtt_port.getValue());
strcpy(mqtt_user, custom_mqtt_user.getValue());
strcpy(mqtt_pass, custom_mqtt_pass.getValue());
strcpy(mqtt_topic, custom_mqtt_topic.getValue());
```

Now that we have received all necessary parameters from the web page, save them to the file config.json. This file is read when the ESP8266 starts:

```
if (saveConfig) {
  Serial.println("saving config");
  DynamicJsonBuffer jsonBuffer;
  JsonObject& json = jsonBuffer.createObject();
  json["mqtt_server"] = mqtt_server;
  json["mqtt_port"]   = mqtt_port;
  json["mqtt_user"]   = mqtt_user;
  json["mqtt_pass"]   = mqtt_pass;
  json["mqtt_topic"]  = mqtt_topic;

  File configFile = SPIFFS.open("/config.json", "w");
  if (!configFile) {
    Serial.println(F("failed to open config file for writing"));
  }

  json.printTo(Serial);
  json.printTo(configFile);
  configFile.close();
  //end save
}
```

Now that the ESP8266 is connected to the Wi-Fi network, the only thing left is to connect to the MQTT broker with the credentials from the `config.json` file and subscribe to a topic:

```
    Serial.println(F("My IP address: "));
    Serial.println(WiFi.localIP());
    //connect to mqtt server
    client.setServer(mqtt_server, atoi(mqtt_port));
    client.setCallback(mqtt_callback);
    if (client.connect(dev_name , mqtt_user, mqtt_pass))
    {
        Serial.println(F("Connected to MQTT broker"));
  Serial.println(F("Subscribe to your mqtt_topic now"));
    }


}

void loop() {
   // put your main code to runin loop
client.loop();
   }
```

In conclusion, this is what you can do with the `WiFiManager` library; create a captive portal that allows you to set up your ESP8266 with Wi-Fi credentials and custom parameters. You can use this library in any project where you would like to give users ability to configure their ESPs with different values.

ESP8266 and Infrared communication

In the previous chapters the ESP866 has been controlling relays, reading temperature and humidity, but not all the appliances around the house can be controlled with a relay. There are some of them that can be controlled using the infrared like TV or air-conditioning Now let's see how we can use ESP8266 to turn on/off a Panasonic TV. This can be extended to other TV brands by modifying the addresses and values.

Hardware components

To complete this project you will need:

- ESP8266
- Infrared LEDs (maybe from an old remote)
- Some 100-ohm resistors (depending on the number of your infrared LEDs, one per LED)
- One 1-Kilo Ohm resistor
- One 2N2222 NPN transistor

Use the following schematic for the hardware part of this project:

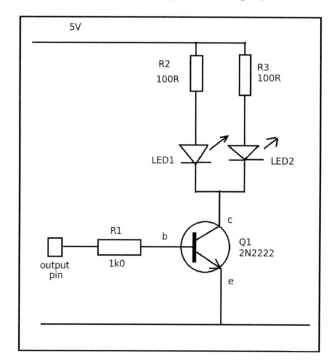

Connect the output pin to the GPIO 12 from the ESP8266 the ground to the GND pin, and 5V to 5V from your ESP.

Software and libraries for this project

First let's install the library `IRremoteESP8266`. For that go to **Sketch** | **Include Library** | **Manage Libraries...** and search for `IRremoteESP8266` library like in the following screenshot:

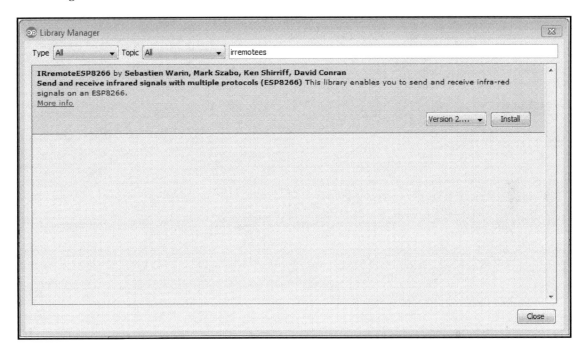

After the library is installed and the connections to the ESP are done, let's use the following code to send over an MQTT topic a command to open or close a Panasonic TV. Since the same Infrared command is used to power on or power off, you just need to receive something on the MQTT topic to send an infrared command to the TV:

```
#include <ArduinoJson.h>
#include <ESP8266WiFi.h>
#include <ESP8266mDNS.h>
#include <WiFiUdp.h>
#include <PubSubClient.h>
#include <IRremoteESP8266.h>
#include <IRsend.h>

#define PanasonicAddress      0x4004
#define PanasonicPower        0x100BCBD  // Panasonic Power button
```

Add your Wi-Fi and MQTT credentials in the next variables:

```
#define wifi_ssid "YOUR_WIFI_SSID"
#define wifi_password "YOUR_WIFI_PASS"

#define mqtt_server "YOUR_MQTT_SERVER"
#define mqtt_user "YOUR_MQTT_USER"
#define mqtt_password "YOUR_MQTT_PASSWORD"
#define mqtt_port 1883
```

Set the infrared pin to the GPIO12 or D6 on NodeMCU and WeMos boards and the topic on which will receive the messages to turn on/off the TV:

```
#define IR_PIN 12
#define ir_topic "/62/ir/command"

void rx_mqtt_callback(char* topic, byte* payload, unsigned int length);

#define DEBUG false
#define Serial if(DEBUG)Serial
#define DEBUG_OUTPUT Serial

IRsend irsend(IR_PIN); // IR led is connected to GPIO pin
WiFiClient espClient;
PubSubClient client(mqtt_server, mqtt_port, rx_mqtt_callback,espClient);

StaticJsonBuffer<512> jsonDeviceStatus;
JsonObject& jsondeviceStatus = jsonDeviceStatus.createObject();

char dev_name[50];
char json_buffer_status[512];
char my_ip_s[16];
```

Start the Wi-Fi and connect to the Wi-Fi network:

```
void setup_wifi()
{
  delay(10);
  // We start by connecting to a WiFi network
  Serial.println();
  Serial.print("Connecting to ");
  Serial.println(wifi_ssid);

  WiFi.mode(WIFI_STA);
  WiFi.begin(wifi_ssid, wifi_password);
  while (WiFi.status() != WL_CONNECTED) {
    delay(500);
    Serial.print(".");
```

```
    }
    Serial.println("");
    Serial.println("WiFi connected");
    Serial.println("IP address: ");
    Serial.println(WiFi.localIP());
}
```

Connect and reconnect to the MQTT broker. In the event of an error try to reconnect every 5 seconds:

```
void reconnect() {
  // Loop until we're reconnected
  while (!client.connected()) {
    Serial.print("Attempting MQTT connection...");
    if (client.connect(dev_name, mqtt_user, mqtt_password)) {
      Serial.println("connected");
    } else {
      Serial.print("failed, rc=");
      Serial.print(client.state());
      Serial.println(" try again in 5 seconds");
      // Wait 5 seconds before retrying
      delay(5000);
    }
  }
}
```

This is the function that will be called when a message is received from the MQTT broker. Get the message and send the infrared commands to the TV:

```
void rx_mqtt_callback(char* topic, byte* payload, unsigned int length)
{
  //reserve space for incomming message
  StaticJsonBuffer<256> jsonRxMqttBuffer;
  int i = 0;
  char rxj[256];
  Serial.println(dev_name);
Serial.print(F("Topic:"));Serial.println(topic);
  for(i=0;i<length;i++)
  {
    rxj[i] = payload[i];
  }

  Serial.println(rxj);
  JsonObject& root = jsonRxMqttBuffer.parseObject(rxj);
  if (!root.success())
  {
    Serial.println(F("parseObject() failed"));
```

```
        return;
    }

    const char* device_name   = root["device_name"];
    const char* type          = root["type"];
    const char* value         = root["value"];

    Serial.println(device_name);
    Serial.println(type); Serial.println(value);

    sendIR();

    return;
}
```

Here we send the message code to the TV. If it doesn't work the first time, try going closer to the TV. It depends on the quality of your IR LEDs, the number of infrared LEDs, and the ambient light:

```
void sendIR()
{
    int i = 0;
    Serial.print("sendIR for 2 sec");
    for(i=0;i<20; i++)
    {
        irsend.sendPanasonic(PanasonicAddress,PanasonicPower); // This should
turn your TV on and off
        delay(100);
    }
}
void setup()
{
  delay(1000);
  irsend.begin();
  Serial.begin(115200);
  sprintf(dev_name, "ESP_%d", ESP.getChipId());
  setup_wifi();
  client.setServer(mqtt_server, mqtt_port);
  client.connect(dev_name, mqtt_user, mqtt_password);
  client.subscribe(ir_topic);
  if (!client.connected())
  {
    reconnect();
  }
}
void loop() {
  client.loop();
}
```

Now, using the MyMQTT Android application, try to send a command to the `ir_topic` to start or stop the TV.

As you have probably already noticed I didn't use the `WiFiManager` to set up the ESP8266, but this is a very good exercise for you to complete the chapter and the project. Study the LIRC library from Linux and try to find other devices that can be controlled with Infrared and the ESP8266.

Summary

In this chapter you learned how to use `WiFiManager` to set up Wi-Fi and add parameters to the configuration file, saved the received values to the SPIFFS, read the values at startup time, and used them to connect to a MQTT broker. Finally, you sent infrared commands to control additional devices such as an air conditioner, TV, and so on.

5
Using ESP8266 to Build a Security System

We all are interested in knowing what is happening at home when we are not in. Either it is about security or critical elements such as gas, fire, or water. Knowing in the moment when something wrong is happening is vital to minimizing the eventual damage. In this chapter, we will focus on the PIR sensor, but the same principles apply to other sensors, such as moisture, gas, or smoke sensors.

Passive infrared sensor

PIR is the most common sensor used in the indoor and outdoor alarm systems. It is also used in automated doors and automated lights systems.

How PIRs work

The functionality of the PIR sensor is based on radiation emitted by human bodies. Objects generate heat as infrared radiation and those objects include animals and the human body whose radiation is strongest at a wavelength of 9.4 μm.

When a human passes the front of the sensor, the temperature from the PIR sensor point of view changes from the background value to the human value. The sensor detects this change in the infrared radiation and changes its output voltage, signaling the detection.

To increase the sensitivity of the PIR sensor, a Fresnel lens is mounted in front of it. A sensor is in fact a FET transistor with a source pin connected with a pull down to ground. We can see this setup in the following figure:

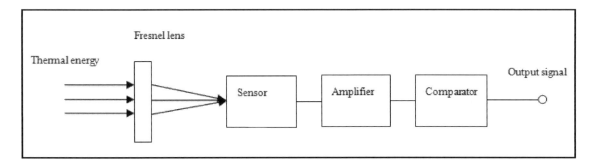

In the following image, we can see a **Fresnel lens** made from plastic:

The sensor itself is located under the dome Fresnel lens and it has an infrared filter in front of it.

Here we can see a **DYP-ME003**:

The module presented here is **DYP-ME003** and it costs you around one dollar per module. Principal characteristics for this module are:

- Angle sensor < 100 degress cone angle
- Board dimensions 32 mm x 24 mm
- Operating temperature -17 to 70 degrees Celsius

- Output level High 3.3 V / Low 0 V
- Operating voltage 4.5-20 V
- Adjustable delay time of 5 to 200 seconds
- Selectable trigger repeated / non repeated trigger

On the module there are two variable resistors that allow you to modify two things:

- **Sensitivity**: This is basically the distance from where the sensor will sense a person. Rotate clockwise to adjust the distance and the sensing range increases (about 7 meters); rotate anti-clockwise and the sensing range decreases to about 3 meters.
- **Time**: If you rotate a potentiometer clockwise it will increase the time when the output is held in high delay (about 300 S), the other way and the time decrease to about five seconds.

Testing the PIR module

For now, let's test the PIR module to check that it is working. In order to achieve this you will need:

- An ESP8266 module (NodeMCU, WeMos, or an other board)
- A PIR module
- A Breadboard
- Wires

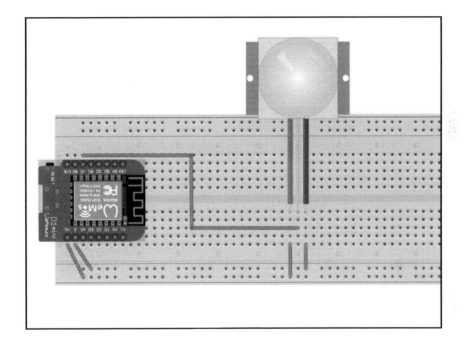

For the software part use the following sketch:

- Define the PIR as it will be connected to the **D7** pin, set the `pirState` to `LOW` assuming that the PIR is OFF, and set the current state to `0`:

```
#define PIN_PIR   D7
int pirState = LOW;
int current_value = 0;
```

- During setup we will declare the **D7** pin where the PIR is connected to an input pin:

```
void setup() {
  pinMode(PIN_PIR, INPUT);
  Serial.begin(115200);
}
```

Now continually monitor the `PIN_PIR` and expect a change to its state. If a change occurs then print on to the serial console the message: `Sensor detected motion!` and when it timeouts the message: `Motion ended...` and change the `pirState` to `LOW`:

```
void loop(){
  current_value = digitalRead(PIN_PIR);
  if (current_value == HIGH) {
    if (pirState == LOW) {
      Serial.println(F("Sensor detected motion!"));
      // We only want to print on the output change, not state
      pirState = HIGH;
    }
  }
  else
  {
    if (pirState == HIGH){
      Serial.println(F("Motion ended..."));
      pirState = LOW;
    }
  }
}
```

As we can see, this sketch is just for testing the PIR so you can play and configure the sensitivity and the timing that you want for your project. To use this sensor just for triggering on or off a light you need to add a relay.

If you want to add a relay to light a lamp on or off when you enter a room, you need to add a relay and change the code a bit:

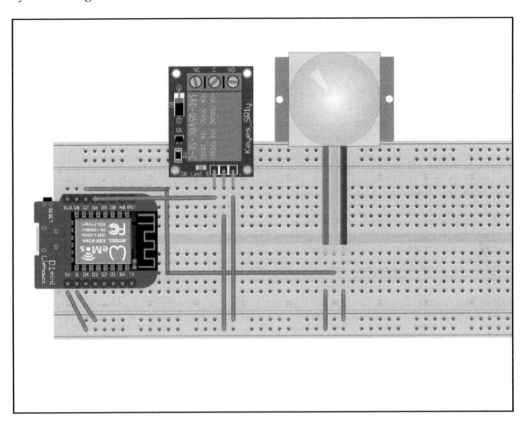

Now the code for adding the relay will be:

```
#define PIN_PIR   D7  //GPIO13
#define RELAY_PIN D6 //GPIO12
int pirState = LOW;
int current_value = 0;
```

Just set the RELAY_PIN as an output pin:

```
void setup() {
  pinMode(PIN_PIR, INPUT);
  pinMode(RELAY_PIN, OUTPUT);
  Serial.begin(115200);
}
```

If the motion is detected, trigger the relay and turn on the lamp. Stop the lamp through the relay when motion is ended:

```
void loop(){
  current_value = digitalRead(PIN_PIR);
  if (current_value == HIGH) {
    if (pirState == LOW) {
      Serial.println(F("Sensor detected motion!"));
      // We only want to print on the output change, not state
      pirState = HIGH;
      digitalWrite(RELAY_PIN,HIGH);
    }
  }
  else
  {
    if (pirState == HIGH){
      Serial.println(F("Motion ended.."));
      pirState = LOW;
      digitalWrite(RELAY_PIN,LOW);
    }
  }
}
```

After compiling and flashing the software, try to move in front of the sensor. In the serial monitor you will see messages that the motion was detected and you will also hear the mechanical relay clicks. If you wired a lamp to the relay, the lamp should go on or off:

Connecting the PIR module to the internet

Everything that we did until now can also be achieved with an Arduino, so where is the value added by the ESP8266? Well, what if you receive a notification as an email and a sound on your phone when a motion is detected at home. Also, you can later combine the detected motion with turning on lights, the TV, or turning on an alarm siren.

In order to do this, we will use a library named `blynk` that can be downloaded from the following link:

`https://github.com/blynkkk/blynk-library` or their mobile application.

Now we shall see how to set it up:

1. First let's download and install the library:

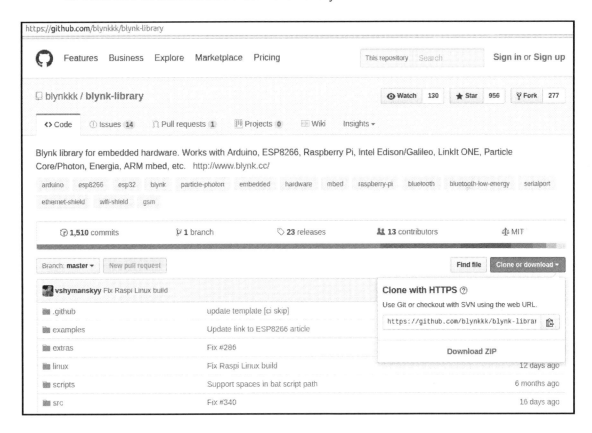

2. Click the **Download ZIP** button. Then go to **Sketch | Include Library | Add .ZIP library...**:

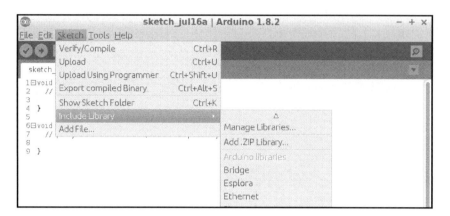

3. Locate the downloaded ZIP file and install the library.

It's time now to install the Android application so we can use it later:

1. Go to Google Play Store and search for `Blynk - Arduino, ESP8266, Rpi,` and install the application:

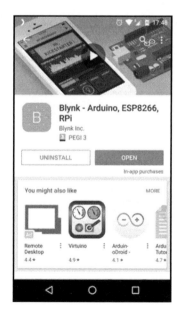

2. Let's focus first on the Android application. Open the application and create an account in the Blynk application:

3. After that, click on **New Project**, set the project name, the hardware type to **ESP8266**, the theme for your application - dark or light, and continue by pressing the **Create** button. The project is created and an email with a token is sent to your email address used for registration. Also, this token can be found later in the **Project Settings** tab:

4. Now the project is created, the token is on the email and we are in the main screen application from where we can add LEDs and notifications on to it. In order to do that press the **+** icon:

5. After you have added all the elements, the main screen of your application needs to look like this:

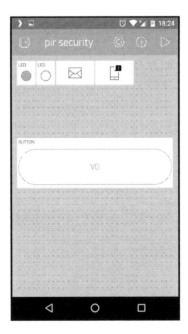

6. Now it is time to configure the LEDs to some virtual pins (**V1** and **V2**), add the email address where the notification will be sent, and set up the sound that will be played by your phone if the device is going offline or a new notification is sent by the Blynk cloud server:

Virtual LED 1:

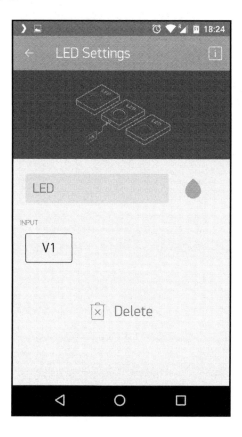

The **Virtual LED 2**:

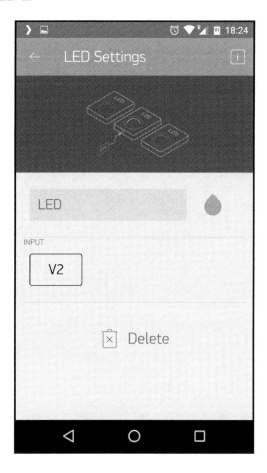

The **Email Settings**:

The **Notification Settings**:

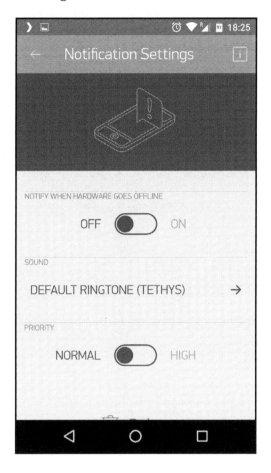

In this moment, the application is ready to be started. If you want to skip all these steps for creating the elements, you can scan the following QR code that will add and set up everything for you. You will just need to change the email address in the email notification element.

The ESP8266 PIR security code

For the ESP8266 and PIR module to work with the defined Blynk application, it includes the Blynk header, the Simple timer, and defines the BLYNK_PRINT as serial for debugging purposes. You need to run the following code:

```
#define BLYNK_PRINT Serial
#include <ESP8266WiFi.h>
#include <BlynkSimpleEsp8266.h>
#include <SimpleTimer.h>
```

Go to the Mobile application and then to **Project Settings** and email yourself the app_token:

```
char app_token[] = "TOKEN_FROM_EMAIL";
SimpleTimer timer;
char ssid[] = "YOUR_WIFI_NETWORK";
char pass[] = "YOUR_PASSWORD";
int state;
int counter=0;
int flag=1;
WidgetLED led1(V1);
WidgetLED pirLED(V2);
```

This is the `timer` function that will be called every second to check the status of the PIR pin. All the logic for the ESP8266 application is in this function:

```
void timer_ev()
{
  counter = counter+1;
  if(counter==5)
  {
    pirLED.off();
    counter=0;
    flag = 1;
  }
  int pirStatus = digitalRead(D7);
  if (pirStatus)
  {
    if (flag == 1)
    {
        Serial.println(F("Sensor detected motion!"));
        Blynk.email("bcatalin@gmail.com","Subject: Security alert!",
"Movement detected!");
        Blynk.notify("Security alert! Someone is in the house!");
        digitalWrite(D4, LOW);
        led1.on();
        pirLED.on();
        flag=2;
    }
  }
}
```

Set up the Blynk with the mobile application token, and start the Wi-Fi connection with the `ssid` and `pass` for the router. You can modify the Wi-Fi setup using the `WiFiManager` so as not to hardcode the values in the code. Also, you can add the MQTT `PubSubClient` library and send Mosquitto a JSON message on a specific topic so that other devices are subscribed to receive the message. For example, you build a siren that will subscribe to the alarm topic, where the module will publish the alarm event. By receiving the alarm message the siren can start its horn. If a light system is subscribing to the alarm topic on receiving the alarm message it can start all the lights in the house:

```
void setup()
{
  Serial.begin(115200);
  Blynk.begin(app_token, ssid, pass);
  pinMode(D4, OUTPUT);
  timer.setInterval(1000L, timer_ev);
}
BLYNK_WRITE(V0)
{
```

```
    state = param.asInt();
    if (state == 1){
      digitalWrite(D4, LOW);
      led1.on();
    }
    else {
      digitalWrite(D4, HIGH);
      led1.off();
    }
  }
```

In the `loop` function, just run the `timer` and `Blynk`:

```
void loop()
{
  Blynk.run();
  timer.run();
}
```

Now move yourself in front of the sensor and you will start receiving messages from the Blynk application on your mobile. Also check the Serial Monitor for messages:

And the message received on the phone will be:

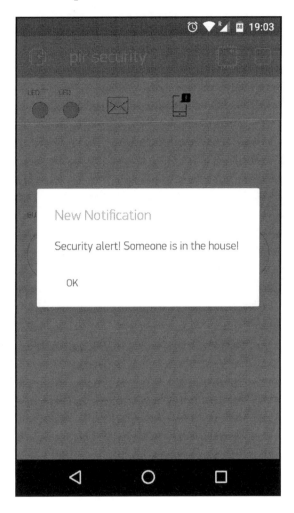

Please notice that the interval for sending messages on Blynk is 15 seconds and also that the maximum number of emails for Gmail is 500 per day.

Summary

Now you can build a security system in no time, but the security is not limited to PIR sensors, you can add other sensors to it, such as CO_2 or gas, or sensors for detecting water leaks or smoke, and you can create a dependency between them. For example, if you have a broken pipe in the house and the water leak sensor detects water you will be notified in the Blynk application, but also another ESP8266 that is subscribing to the leak topic can close the main valve so the damage is limited by the time you arrive home.

6
Securing Your Data

In *Chapter 2*, *Building and Configuring Your Own MQTT Server*, you have learned about the MQTT protocol, how a topic is constructed, and how to install and configure a mosquitto broker. At that time, you used a local configuration file to add a user and a password to be used as an authentication method for a local broker. How about the time the packets are travelling from your ESP8266 module to a cloud mosquitto instance? To encrypt the packets, you need to enable security on mosquitto and send encrypted packets from your ESP8266.

Enabling encryption on mosquitto

To enable encryption on mosquitto, you need first to have certificates. You can buy them from a company that is issuing certificates or you can generate them yourself as self-sign certificates.

Installing the openssl package

First, verify that you have the `openssl` package installed and it has a newer version (1.0.2g), as seen in the following screenshot:

```
catalin@lubuntuBIG:~$ openssl version
OpenSSL 1.0.2g  1 Mar 2016
catalin@lubuntuBIG:~$
catalin@lubuntuBIG:~$
catalin@lubuntuBIG:~$
```

If you don't have `openssl` installed you need to install it first, using the following command:

```
sudo apt install openssl on Ubuntu
```

Or use the following command:

```
yum install openssl on CentOS/Redhat
```

Generating your own certificates

First go to `/etc/mosquitto/certs` and issue the following command:

```
sudo openssl req -x509 -newkey rsa:1024 -keyout ca.crt -out cert.crt -days
9999
```

You will then be invited to fill some details, as seen in the following screenshot, about the owner of the certificate, such as country of residence, state, company, city, email address, and the most important one is the **Fully Qualified Domain Name (FQDN)**. That needs to be your server domain or your server IP address if you don't have a domain name for it:

```
catalin@lubuntuBIG:/etc/mosquitto/certs$
catalin@lubuntuBIG:/etc/mosquitto/certs$ sudo openssl req -x509 -newkey rsa:1024 -keyout ca.crt -out cert.crt -days 9999
Generating a 1024 bit RSA private key
.....................................++++++
........................................++++++
writing new private key to 'ca.crt'
Enter PEM pass phrase:
Verifying - Enter PEM pass phrase:
-----
You are about to be asked to enter information that will be incorporated
into your certificate request.
What you are about to enter is what is called a Distinguished Name or a DN.
There are quite a few fields but you can leave some blank
For some fields there will be a default value,
If you enter '.', the field will be left blank.
-----
Country Name (2 letter code) [AU]:RO
State or Province Name (full name) [Some-State]:Bucharest
Locality Name (eg, city) []:Bucharest
Organization Name (eg, company) [Internet Widgits Pty Ltd]:HalogenSoftware
Organizational Unit Name (eg, section) []:IoT Dep
Common Name (e.g. server FQDN or YOUR name) []:iotcentral.eu
Email Address []:email@server.com
catalin@lubuntuBIG:/etc/mosquitto/certs$
catalin@lubuntuBIG:/etc/mosquitto/certs$
```

When you are asked about a passphrase you need to enter one that is more than four characters. Don't worry, in the next step we will delete it from the certificate.

The result of the preceding command should be two files located in the
`/etc/mosquitto/certs` directory:

```
catalin@lubuntuBIG:/etc/mosquitto/certs$
catalin@lubuntuBIG:/etc/mosquitto/certs$ ll
total 16
drwxr-xr-x 2 root root 4096 okt  7 17:40 ./
drwxr-xr-x 5 root root 4096 okt  7 17:29 ../
-rw-r--r-- 1 root root 1041 okt  7 17:30 ca.crt
-rw-r--r-- 1 root root 1107 okt  7 17:30 cert.crt
catalin@lubuntuBIG:/etc/mosquitto/certs$
catalin@lubuntuBIG:/etc/mosquitto/certs$
catalin@lubuntuBIG:/etc/mosquitto/certs$
```

The following command removes the previous passphrase and generates a new file:

```
sudo openssl rsa -in ca.crt -out newca.pem
```

Input file for this command is the `ca.crt` and it will produce a file names `newca.pem` with
the passphrase removed. We can see this in the following screenshot:

```
catalin@lubuntuBIG:/etc/mosquitto/certs$
catalin@lubuntuBIG:/etc/mosquitto/certs$
catalin@lubuntuBIG:/etc/mosquitto/certs$ sudo openssl rsa -in ca.crt -out newca.pem
Enter pass phrase for ca.crt:
writing RSA key
catalin@lubuntuBIG:/etc/mosquitto/certs$
catalin@lubuntuBIG:/etc/mosquitto/certs$
catalin@lubuntuBIG:/etc/mosquitto/certs$
```

In the end, you should have three files in `/etc/mosquitto/certs`:

```
catalin@lubuntuBIG:/etc/mosquitto/certs$ ll
total 20
drwxr-xr-x 2 root root 4096 okt  7 17:43 ./
drwxr-xr-x 5 root root 4096 okt  7 17:29 ../
-rw-r--r-- 1 root root 1041 okt  7 17:30 ca.crt
-rw-r--r-- 1 root root 1107 okt  7 17:30 cert.crt
-rw-r--r-- 1 root root  887 okt  7 17:43 newca.pem
catalin@lubuntuBIG:/etc/mosquitto/certs$
catalin@lubuntuBIG:/etc/mosquitto/certs$
```

Note: In the mosquitto configuration you will need only two of the three
files `cert.crt` and `newca.pem`. Make sure that the `ca.crt` is stored
securely outside of your server. Make sure that the certificates are
accessed only by the mosquitto user. The mosquitto broker in production
should also be started by the mosquitto user and not be the root user.

Now that you have the right files with the certificates let's configure mosquitto to take them into account. If you want to have two ports unsecure such as 1883 and for the WebSockets connection 9004, you can add, for example, 8883 as a secure port and 9883 as a **WebSocket Secure (WSS)** port.

To configure mosquitto you need to edit the configuration file mosquitto.conf located in /etc/mosquitto/. The new content of the file should be:

```
catalin@lubuntuBIG:/etc/mosquitto$
catalin@lubuntuBIG:/etc/mosquitto$
catalin@lubuntuBIG:/etc/mosquitto$ more mosquitto.conf

listener 1883
protocol mqtt
listener 9004
protocol websockets
allow_anonymous true

# MQTT over TLS/SSL
listener 8883
cafile /etc/mosquitto/certs/cert.crt
certfile /etc/mosquitto/certs/cert.crt
keyfile /etc/mosquitto/certs/newca.pem
tls_version tlsv1

# WebSockets over TLS/SSL
listener 9883
protocol websockets
cafile /etc/mosquitto/certs/cert.crt
certfile /etc/mosquitto/certs/cert.crt
keyfile /etc/mosquitto/certs/newca.pem

pid_file /var/run/mosquitto.pid

persistence true
persistence_location /var/lib/mosquitto/

log_dest file /var/log/mosquitto/mosquitto.log

include_dir /etc/mosquitto/conf.d

catalin@lubuntuBIG:/etc/mosquitto$
catalin@lubuntuBIG:/etc/mosquitto$
```

Restart your mosquitto service to start with the new configuration, using the following command:

```
sudo service mosquitto restart
```

Now you can check that mosquitto has been started correctly and you don't have errors in the `mosquitto.conf`, by looking to `/var/log/mosquitto/mosquitto.log`:

```
1507382754: mosquitto version 1.4.8 terminating
1507382756: mosquitto version 1.4.8 (build date Tue, 23 May 2017 22:14:40 +0100) starting
1507382756: Config loaded from /etc/mosquitto/mosquitto.conf.
1507382756: Opening ipv4 listen socket on port 1883.
1507382756: Opening ipv6 listen socket on port 1883.
1507382756: Opening websockets listen socket on port 9004.
1507382756: Opening ipv4 listen socket on port 8883.
1507382756: Opening ipv6 listen socket on port 8883.
1507382756: Opening websockets listen socket on port 9883.
```

If there are no errors, you can proceed to connect your clients to the new secure ports.

Securing a connection between ESP8266 and an MQTT broker

If you don't want to have your own broker, but you want a secure MQTT connection you can use a cloud MQTT instance, such as `http://iotcentral.eu`.

First create an account on `iotcentral.eu` and confirm your email address. After that you can log in to `iotcentral.eu` and get your private assigned topic. It is an eight character code, such as `c5c05211`, and this code needs to precede all of your topics as follows:

```
c5c05211/living/temperature
```

No matter if you publish or subscribe. The following code connects to the Wi-Fi and then establishes a secure connection to the `iotcentral.eu` cloud MQTT over port `8883`. Every message sent to the `iotcentral.eu` broker is received back like a loopback.

Included header files are the `ESP8266WiFi` and the `PubSubClient` MQTT class:

```
#include <ESP8266WiFi.h>
#include <PubSubClient.h>
```

GPIO `12` will be used later to blink a LED every time a message is received and GPIO `13` will be changed to `HIGH` every time a message with content `1` is received, and to `LOW` if the message payload is `0`:

```
#define PIN_12 12
#define PIN_13 13
```

Define here the values for the Wi-Fi network, SSID, and password, along with the MQTT server used (in this example `iotcentral.eu` was used, but you can use a local one), username, password, and base topic (we need to take this from `iotcentral.eu` in your account):

```
const char* ssid = "YOUR_WIFI_SSID";
const char* password = "YOUR_WIFI_PASSWORD";
const char* mqtt_server = "iotcentral.eu";
const char* mqtt_username = "email@email.com"; //email address used on
iotcentral.eu
const char* mqtt_password = "*******"; //your password used on
iotcentral.eu
#define MQTT_CLIENT_ID          "ESP_%06X"
#define BASE_TOPIC "c5c05211" //get it from iotcentral.eu
char dev_name[11];
```

If in the other examples in the book, the `WiFiClient` class was used for non-secure connection, here the `WiFiClientSecure` class will be used to create the `espClient` object:

```
WiFiClientSecure espClient;
PubSubClient client(espClient);
long lastMsg = 0;
char msg[50];
int value = 0;
```

In the `setup` function, we will connect the ESP8266 to the provided Wi-Fi network and write into the client object the MQTT server that will be used and the port. In previous examples, port 1883 was used. The broker is listening on port 8883 for a secure connection to the 8883 port is provided:

```
void setup()
{
  pinMode(PIN_12, OUTPUT);
  digitalWrite(PIN_12, LOW);
  pinMode(PIN_13, OUTPUT);
  digitalWrite(PIN_13, LOW);
  sprintf(dev_name, MQTT_CLIENT_ID, ESP.getChipId());
  Serial.begin(115200);
  setup_wifi();
  client.setServer(mqtt_server, 8883);
  client.setCallback(callback);
}
```

Use the following to start the Wi-Fi connection:

```
void setup_wifi() {
  delay(10);
  // First connect to WiFi network
  Serial.print("Connecting to ");
  Serial.println(ssid);
  WiFi.begin(ssid, password);
  while (WiFi.status() != WL_CONNECTED) {
    delay(500);
    Serial.print(".");
  }
  Serial.println("");
  Serial.println("WiFi connected. My IP address: ");
  Serial.println(WiFi.localIP());
}
```

This is the `callback` function that is called every time a message is received from the broker. If an LED is connected on the GPIO 12 then it will light for 50 ms every time a message is received:

```
void callback(char* topic, byte* payload, unsigned int length) {
  digitalWrite(PIN_12,HIGH);
  delay(50);
  digitalWrite(PIN_12,LOW);
  Serial.print("Message arrived [");
  Serial.print(topic);
  Serial.print("] ");
  for (int i = 0; i < length; i++) {
    Serial.print((char)payload[i]);
  }
  Serial.println("");
  // Switch ON the LED connected to PIN_13 if an '1' message was received
on any topic
  if ((char)payload[0] == '1') {
    digitalWrite(PIN_13, HIGH);    // Turn the LED on
  }
  else if ( (char)payload[0] == '0')
  {
    digitalWrite(PIN_13, LOW);
  }
}
```

If the connection with the broker is lost, try to reconnect. If you want to make this more robust, you can also verify the Wi-Fi connection and try to reconnect to the Wi-Fi router and then to the MQTT broker:

```
void reconnect() {
  // Loop until we're reconnected
  while (!client.connected()) {
    Serial.print("Start MQTT connection...");
    if (client.connect(dev_name, mqtt_username, mqtt_password)) {
      Serial.print("connected to MQTT broker");
      Serial.println(mqtt_server);
      client.subscribe(BASE_TOPIC"/#");
    } else {
      Serial.print("Failed to connect. Error code: ");
      Serial.println(client.state());
      Serial.println(" try again in 5 seconds");
      // Disconnect and wait 5 seconds before retrying
      client.disconnect();
      delay(5000);
    }
  }
}
```

The main loop code checks if the ESP8266 is still connected to the `iotcentral.eu` MQTT broker. In case of failure, it will try to reconnect. Every second increment a value and publish this value in a message to the broker:

```
void loop() {
  if (!client.connected()) {
    Serial.println("Reconnect to the broker....");
    reconnect();
  }
  client.loop();

  long now = millis();
  if (now - lastMsg > 1000) {
    lastMsg = now;
    ++value;
    snprintf (msg, 75, "Sending message #%ld", value);
    Serial.print("Send to MQTT broker message: ");
    Serial.println(msg);
    client.publish(BASE_TOPIC"/outTopic", msg);
  }
}
```

Because in the `reconnect` function, we subscribed to:

```
client.subscribe(BASE_TOPIC"/#");
```

and we are publishing to:

```
client.publish(BASE_TOPIC"/outTopic", msg);
```

Every time a message is sent the broker will send it back. Open the serial terminal and you will see the following messages:

```
Message arrived [c5c05211/outTopic] Sending message #2048
Send to MQTT broker message: Sending message #2049
Message arrived [c5c05211/outTopic] Sending message #2049
Send to MQTT broker message: Sending message #2050
Message arrived [c5c05211/outTopic] Sending message #2050
Send to MQTT broker message: Sending message #2051
Message arrived [c5c05211/outTopic] Sending message #2051
Send to MQTT broker message: Sending message #2052
Message arrived [c5c05211/outTopic] Sending message #2052
Send to MQTT broker message: Sending message #2053
Message arrived [c5c05211/outTopic] Sending message #2053
Send to MQTT broker message: Sending message #2054
Message arrived [c5c05211/outTopic] Sending message #2054
```

Working offline

If your data is more sensitive and you don't want to share it across the Wi-Fi network or you don't have Wi-Fi connectivity, a solution is to store your data on an SD card.

Let's see how data can be stored on an SD card.

Necessary hardware that will be used:

- Wemos D1 mini:

- microSD card shield:

- microSD card:

Since the microSD card is a shield for the Wemos D1 mini, it is easy to stack them; you just need to solder the pins that are coming into the package:

Let's determine the size of the SD card with the following sketch.

Include the `SPI.h` and the `SD` library:

```
#include <SPI.h>
#include <SD.h>
```

Set up variables using the SD utility library functions:

```
Sd2Card card;
SdVolume volume;
SdFile root;
const int chipSelect = D8;
```

In the `setup` function, we will determine if the card is inserted or not and the card details will be read over SPI:

```
void setup()
{
  Serial.begin(115200);
  Serial.print("\nInitializing SD card...");
```

Use the initialization code from the utility libraries:

```
    if (!card.init(SPI_HALF_SPEED, chipSelect)) {
    Serial.println("initialization failed. Things to check:");
    Serial.println("* is a card inserted?");
    Serial.println("* is your wiring correct?");
    Serial.println("* did you change the chipSelect pin to match your
shield or module?");
    return;
  } else {
    Serial.println("Wiring is correct and a card is present.");
  }
  // print the type of card
  Serial.print("\nCard type: ");
  switch (card.type()) {
    case SD_CARD_TYPE_SD1:
      Serial.println("SD1");
      break;
    case SD_CARD_TYPE_SD2:
      Serial.println("SD2");
      break;
    case SD_CARD_TYPE_SDHC:
      Serial.println("SDHC");
      break;
    default:
      Serial.println("Unknown");
```

```
  }
  // Now we will try to open the 'volume'/'partition' - it should be FAT16
or FAT32
  if (!volume.init(card)) {
    Serial.println("Could not find FAT16/FAT32 partition.\nMake sure you've
formatted the card");
    return;
  }
  // print the type and size of the first FAT-type volume
  uint32_t volumesize;
  Serial.print("\nVolume type is FAT");
  Serial.println(volume.fatType(), DEC);
  Serial.println();
  volumesize = volume.blocksPerCluster();    // clusters are collections of
blocks
  volumesize *= volume.clusterCount();       // we'll have a lot of
clusters
  volumesize *= 512;                              // SD card blocks are
always 512 bytes
  Serial.print("Volume size (bytes): ");
  Serial.println(volumesize);
  Serial.print("Volume size (Kbytes): ");
  volumesize /= 1024;
  Serial.println(volumesize);
  Serial.print("Volume size (Mbytes): ");
  volumesize /= 1024;
  Serial.println(volumesize);
  Serial.println("\nFiles found on the card (name, date and size in bytes):
");
  root.openRoot(volume);
  // list all files in the card with date and size
  root.ls(LS_R | LS_DATE | LS_SIZE);
}
```

In the `loop` function there is nothing to do, since determining the card type and its properties has been done in the `setup` function:

```
void loop()
{
  // nothing happens after setup
}
```

The output of the serial console will show the card type, card size in bytes, kilobytes and megabytes, and if there are some files on the card, the name and the size of them:

```
Card type: SD2

Volume type is FAT16

Volume size (bytes): 987463680
Volume size (Kbytes): 964320
Volume size (Mbytes): 941

Files found on the card (name, date and size in bytes):
DATALOG.TXT    2000-01-01 01:00:00 4978
```

You can also use a bigger SDHC card or a FAT32 card:

```
Initializing SD card...Wiring is correct and a card is present.

Card type: SDHC

Volume type is FAT32

Volume size (bytes): 2670723072
Volume size (Kbytes): 2608128
Volume size (Mbytes): 2547

Files found on the card (name, date and size in bytes):
```

Saving data on the SD card

Let's assume that now you need to save data to the SD card, data that can be used later offline in a PC.

Let's attach a DHT22 like we did in Chapter 3, *Building a Home Thermostat with the ESP8266,* and read its value and log it in file on the microSD card.

Using the same libraries for the SPI and SD card:

```
#include <SPI.h>
#include <SD.h>
#include <DHT.h>
const int chipSelect = D8;
```

Define the DHT type, since the library can work with DHT11 and DHT22:

```
#define DHTTYPE DHT22
#define DHTPIN  4
#define DEV_TYPE  "dht"
DHT dht(DHTPIN, DHTTYPE, 11);
float humidity, temp_f;  // Values read from sensor
```

Define the function that will read the temperature and update the global variables humidity and temp_f with the humidity and temperature:

```
void gettemperature()
{
  int runs=0;
  do {
      delay(2000);
      temp_f = dht.readTemperature(false);
      humidity = dht.readHumidity();

      if(runs > 0)
          Serial.println("##Failed to read from DHT sensor! ###");
      runs++;
    }
    while(isnan(temp_f) && isnan(humidity));
}
```

Initialize the SD card and do the first reading for humidity and temperature:

```
void setup()
{
  // Open serial communications and wait for port to open:
  Serial.begin(115200);
  Serial.print("Initializing SD card...");
  // see if the card is present and can be initialized:
  if (!SD.begin(chipSelect)) {
    Serial.println("Card failed, or not present");
    // don't do anything more:
    return;
  }
  Serial.println("card initialized.");
  gettemperature();
}
```

Every three seconds, read the temperature and humidity, opening an existing file and appending the temperature in the DATALOG.TXT file. At the end, close the file:

```
void loop()
{
  // make a string for assembling the data to log:
  String dataString = "";
  gettemperature();
  dataString += String(temp_f);
  // open the file. note that only one file can be open at a time,
  // so you have to close this one before opening another.
  // to write to file you need FILE_WRITE as second parameter.
  // to read from the file SD.open(file_name) should be used.
  File dataFile = SD.open("datalog.txt", FILE_WRITE);
  // if the file is available, write to it:
  if (dataFile)
  {
    dataFile.println(dataString);
    dataFile.close();
    // print to the serial port too:
    Serial.println(dataString);
  }
  // if the file isn't open, pop up an error:
  else {
    Serial.println("error opening datalog.txt");
  }
  delay(3000);
}
```

Check that the microSD card on a PC shows the created file:

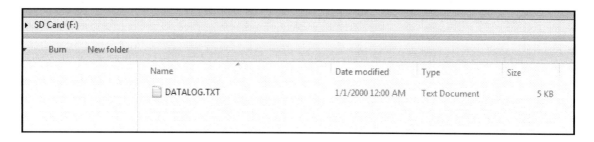

Open the file to view the logged data:

```
 DATALOG.TXT - Notepad
 File   Edit   Format   View   Help
23.50
23.40
23.40
23.30
23.30|
23.30
23.30
23.30
23.30
23.30
23.30
23.30
23.30
23.30
23.30
23.20
23.20
```

If your data is sensitive you can encrypt the data and then write it to the SD card. In case the SD card is lost, no one will be able to see your data.

Summary

Now you can transmit encrypted MQTT messages to an MQTT broker, and from there to another ESP8266 or to a database or a server. Doing this, no one can intercept and alter your data, so your home or your data are secure. Security in IoT is very important nowadays, since there are a lot of devices that are not secured even with a user and a password. If you need to work offline, now you have an entire microSD card to write or read data from it. Using a battery-powered ESP8266 and deep sleep features, now you can log data to a microSD card up to few a months. Encrypt them to be sure that you are the only one that has access to them.

In the next chapter will see how to stream data over a WebSocket connection, data that can be stored in a time series database or displayed as a real-time graphic.

Real-Time Communication

7

All the communication that has been presented until now was based on a request response method, in which one entity was sending a request and an other entity was sending back a response. But there are situations when you need real-time communications between the ESP8266 module and a server, not just transactions. To achieve real-time communication, we will use WebSockets to stream the acceleration values from an acceleration sensor to a server to display them in a real-time graphic, and also to store them in a time-series database.

WebSockets

WebSockets is a communication protocol, providing full-duplex messages, streaming on top of a **Transport Control Protocol (TCP)**. It is standardized by the W3 organizations and it is present on all major browsers (Internet Explorer must be at version 11+). WebSockets enables the communication between a browser and a server and between our module and a server. Through the server, the data from the ESP8266 can arrive in a browser. Another big advantage for WebSockets is the bidirectional communication without creating a new request. Every communication is done on the opened TCP connection.

Protocol details

A WebSocket connection starts as an HTTP connection with the request to upgrade to a `websocket` protocol.

In this case, the client is sending:

```
GET /chat HTTP/1.1
Host: server.example.com
Upgrade: websocket
Connection: Upgrade
Sec-WebSocket-Key: t3JJHjbGL5EzHkh8GBMXGw==
Sec-WebSocket-Protocol: chat, superchat
Sec-WebSocket-Version: 13
Origin: http://example.com
```

And if the server is `websocket` protocol capable, it will respond with:

```
HTTP/1.1 101 Switching Protocols
Upgrade: websocket
Connection: Upgrade
Sec-WebSocket-Accept: ADnfv8rNkTYjSFnn5OPpH2HaGWj=
```

Note that the value for the `Sec-WebSocket-Key` is a random value base64 encoded to avoid caching. The server appends the fixed value `258EAFA5-E914-47DA-95CA-C5AB0DC85B11` on the received value of `Sec-WebSocket-Key` and is doing a SHA1. The result is added to the `Sec-WebSocket-Accept` and sent back to the client. From now on, the communication is established, and server and client can exchange messages.

Streaming data from ESP8266

To stream data from ESP8266 we need first to establish a WebSocket connection between the ESP8266 and a server; data that will be streamed over the WebSocket connection will be the acceleration values for the X, Y and Z axes. ESP8266 will read them from an ADXL345 chip and will send them to a `nodeJS` server. From the server, data can be sent to a connected browser on the same server or can be written to a database for further analysis:

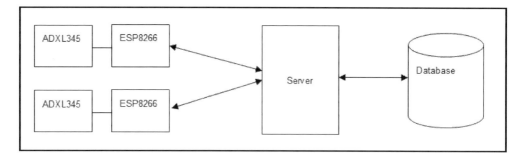

The final circuit can also include a time-series database such as InfluxDb, for storing the values transmitted by the ADXL345.

Adding a database can let you collect various data from multiple acceleration sensors, store them in the database, retrieve them on request to compare them with the current values, or draw nice graphs with the current and historical data.

A server can also react to some values and send alerts (email, SMS) and send data to other ESP8266 modules to react, or to other servers.

ADXL345 accelerometer

Produced by the **Analog Devices (AD)**, it is an ultra-low power 3 axis-accelerometer being capable of high-resolution measurements up to ± 16g. If you plan to measure just the Earth's gravity then ± 2g can be enough for you. For a car movement, ± 4g will be fine but if you want to track an object that suddenly stops you will need ± 16g:

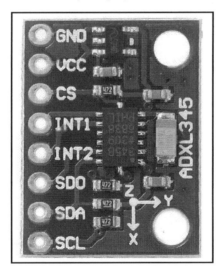

The **ADXL345** can be connected to the ESP8266 over SPI or I2C lines. In our case, we will use the I2C connection. The bus address on which the accelerometer will respond is 0x53.

Pin	Description
GND	Connect to the ground
VCC	VCC 3V3. Some modules accept 5V since they have a voltage drop to 3V3
CS	Chip select. High for I2C and LOW for SPI connection to ESP8266
INT1	Programmable interrupt
INT2	Programmable interrupt
SDO	Serial data out for SPI. For I2C select the bus address
SDA	Serial data for I2C
SCL	Serial clock signal

Connection to the ESP8266

ADXL345 will be connected to the ESP8266 on the I2C bus, which means that only four wires will be used, **VCC**, **GND**, **SDA**, and **SCL**:

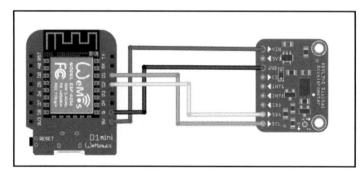

ESP8266 code

Since the sketch has also some extra classes for the WebSocket connection, here the essential part of the `.ino` file will just be shown. For the entire project, please see the following GitHub address:

`https://github.com/bcatalin/esp8266-book/tree/master/Chapter7`.

Necessary included files are:

```
#include "Wire.h"
#include <Adafruit_Sensor.h>
#include <Adafruit_ADXL345_U.h>
#include <FS.h>
#include <ESP8266WiFi.h>
#include "SocketIOClient.h"
#include <DNSServer.h>
#include <ESP8266WebServer.h>
#include <WiFiManager.h>
#include <ArduinoJson.h>
#include <Wire.h>
#include <ESP8266HTTPClient.h>
#include <ESP8266httpUpdate.h>
#include <SPI.h>
```

Instantiate an `accel` object and create a unique identification as a parameter for the class constructor:

```
Adafruit_ADXL345_Unified accel = Adafruit_ADXL345_Unified(121212);
```

Allocate space for the server name or its IP address, and set the default port to `1234`. Later, users will be able to select one during the Wi-Fi setup procedure:

```
char acc_server[40];
char acc_port[6] = "1234";
```

Declare global variables that will be used:

```
#define ACC_CLIENT_ID        "RAM_%06X"
#define INFO Serial.printf
char dev_name[50];
```

Set the `clean_g` to 1 if you want to format the SPIFFS and flash the sketch once again to ESP8266:

```
int clean_g = 0;
//flag for saving data
bool shouldSaveConfig = false;
```

The client object will be used to send and receive data over the websocket protocol. Class implementation is external to this file and will be found in the SocketIOClient.cpp and SocketIOClient.h files:

```
SocketIOClient client;
StaticJsonBuffer<300> jsonBuffer;
extern String RID;
extern String Rname;
//extern String Rcontent;
unsigned long previousMillis = 0;
long interval = 100;
unsigned long lastreply = 0;
unsigned long lastsend = 0;
```

The Callback function for notifying us of the need to save the configuration to config.json file on SPIFFS is:

```
void saveConfigCallback () {
  Serial.println("Should save config");
  shouldSaveConfig = true;
}
```

In the setup() function, it will initialize and set up the ADXL345 chip:

```
void setup()
{
  // put your setup code here, to run once:
  Serial.begin(115200); delay(10);
  Serial.println();
  pinMode(A0, INPUT);
  pinMode(SIGNAL_PIN, OUTPUT); digitalWrite(SIGNAL_PIN, LOW);
```

Initialize the sensor. If the sensor is not connected to the ESP8266 board then wait for it:

```
 if(!accel.begin())
 {
 /* There was a problem detecting the ADXL345 ... check your connections */
 Serial.println("Ooops, no ADXL345 detected ... Check your wiring!");
 while(1);
 }
```

Set the range to whatever is appropriate for your project. ADXL345 can support up to ±16g. Depending on your application, you can choose a different value by changing the SetRange function's parameter:

```
accel.setRange(ADXL345_RANGE_16_G);
// accel.setRange(ADXL345_RANGE_8_G);
```

```
// accel.setRange(ADXL345_RANGE_4_G);
// accel.setRange(ADXL345_RANGE_2_G);
Just for
  if(clean_g)
    SPIFFS.format();
```

Next, read the configuration from the SPIFFS `config.json` file. If the configuration file is not found, then ESP8266 assumes that it is not configured, so it will start itself in access point mode and will wait for the user to set up the Wi-Fi SSID, Wi-Fi password, server name, and server's port, that will be used to connect to:

```
if (SPIFFS.begin())
{
  Serial.println(F("mounted file system"));
  if (SPIFFS.exists("/config.json"))
  {
    //file exists, reading and loading
    Serial.println("reading config file");
    File configFile = SPIFFS.open("/config.json", "r");
    if (configFile) {
      Serial.println("opened config file");
      size_t size = configFile.size();
      // Allocate a buffer to store contents of the file.
      std::unique_ptr<char[]> buf(new char[size]);

      configFile.readBytes(buf.get(), size);
      DynamicJsonBuffer jsonBuffer;
      JsonObject& json = jsonBuffer.parseObject(buf.get());
      json.printTo(Serial);
      if (json.success()) {
        Serial.println(F("\nparsed json"));

        strcpy(acc_server, json["acc_server"]);
        strcpy(acc_port,   json["acc_port"]);
      } else {
        Serial.println(F("failed to load json config"));
      }
    }
  }
} else {
  Serial.println(F("failed to mount FS"));
}
```

Configure the `WiFiManager` with custom fields such as server name and server port, along with the Wi-Fi SSID and Wi-Fi password that will be saved to the SPIFFS in order to connect automatically every time ESP8266 is restarted:

```
WiFiManagerParameter custom_acc_server("server", "RAM IP", acc_server,
40);
WiFiManagerParameter custom_acc_port("port", "RAM port", acc_port, 5);
WiFiManager wifiManager;
wifiManager.setSaveConfigCallback(saveConfigCallback);
wifiManager.addParameter(&custom_acc_server);
wifiManager.addParameter(&custom_acc_port);

if(clean_g)
 wifiManager.resetSettings();
sprintf(dev_name, ACC_CLIENT_ID, ESP.getChipId());
INFO("..DEV:%s \n",dev_name);
if ( !wifiManager.autoConnect(dev_name) )
  {
    Serial.println(F("failed to connect and hit timeout"));
    delay(3000);
    //reset and try again, or maybe put it to deep sleep
    ESP.reset();
    delay(5000);
  }

//if you get here you have connected to the WiFi
Serial.println("connected...yeey :)");
//read updated parameters
strcpy(acc_server, custom_acc_server.getValue());
strcpy(acc_port, custom_acc_port.getValue());
```

Now we have all the information that will be saved to the SPIFFS. This part will only be called the first time the ESP8266 is configured. Information introduced will be persistent since it is now saved and retrieved on every boot:

```
if (shouldSaveConfig)
{
  Serial.println("saving config");
  DynamicJsonBuffer jsonBuffer;
  JsonObject& json = jsonBuffer.createObject();
  json["acc_server"] = acc_server;
  json["acc_port"]    = acc_port;
  File configFile = SPIFFS.open("/config.json", "w");
  if (!configFile) {
    Serial.println("failed to open config file for writing");
  }
```

```
      json.printTo(Serial);
      json.printTo(configFile);
      configFile.close();
  }
```

Now we'll connect to the server, and after that we will send a connection message that contains our unique identification derived from the MAC address of the ESP8266.

The server can use this message to identify the ESP8266 and to dynamically construct some web interface. In this case, if the server receives a *connection* message it will construct a graphic that will show the received values for all the three axes in real time:

```
  if (!client.connect(acc_server, atoi(acc_port) ))
    {
      Serial.println(F("connection failed"));
      return;
    }
  if (client.connected())
    {
      client.sendJSON("connection", "{\"acc_id\":\"" + String(dev_name) + "\"
}" );
    }
  }
```

In the main loop we'll:

- Read the values for the acceleration every interval and will construct a JSON message that will be sent to the server.
- Check for any incoming messages from the server. Remember that the websocket is a duplex protocol. You can also control the ESP8266 from the server; you can set some parameters, reboot the ESP8266, trigger a certain GPIO, or even reset the ESP8266 to its default values by formatting the SPIFFS.
- Check the state of the connection and if it is necessary, reconnect to the server.

Also, in the loop() function will check the state of the connection and if necessary, reconnect to the server if the connection has been lost:

```
void loop()
{
  unsigned long currentMillis = millis();
  if (currentMillis - previousMillis > interval)
  {
    previousMillis = currentMillis;

    sensors_event_t event;
    accel.getEvent(&event);
```

```
        String acc_data;
        StaticJsonBuffer<100> jsonDeviceStatus;
        JsonObject& jsondeviceStatus = jsonDeviceStatus.createObject();
        jsondeviceStatus["device_name"] = dev_name;
        jsondeviceStatus["x"]           = event.acceleration.x;//x;
        jsondeviceStatus["y"]           = event.acceleration.y;//y;
        jsondeviceStatus["z"]           = event.acceleration.z;//z;

        jsondeviceStatus.printTo(acc_data);
        client.sendJSON("JSON", acc_data);
    }
```

Check for any incoming messages from the server:

```
    if(client.monitor())
    {
        lastreply = millis();
```

If the ESP8266 receives a message named `welcome`, it will respond with a message named `connection` and with its unique ID:

```
    if(strcmp(String(RID).c_str(), "welcome") == 0)
    {
      client.sendJSON("connection", "{\"acc_id\":\"" + String(dev_name) + "\"
    }" );
    }
    if(RID != "")
    {
      Serial.print(F("Message: ")); Serial.println(RID);
```

If the received message is `resetModule`, then the EPS8266 will reset itself. A lot of messages can be added here, to change the status of a GPIO, to read a GPIO status, to read the value from `A0`, or to write a PWM to a GPIO:

```
    if(strcmp(String(RID).c_str(), "resetModule") == 0)
    {       //reset the module          delay(1000);          ESP.reset();
      } }
    }
```

Check the connection with the server and if it is necessary, reconnect to it:

```
    if (!client.connected())
    {
        Serial.println("LOOP: Client not connected, try to reconnect");
        client.connect(acc_server, atoi(acc_port) );
        while(!client.connected())
        {
          client.connect(acc_server,atoi(acc_port));
```

```
      delay(1000);
    }
    client.sendJSON("connection", "{\"acc_id\":\"" + String(dev_name) +
"\" }" );
  }
}
```

Server for the WebSocket connection? for the server part, I've chosen Node.JS and ExpressJS. The code for the server can be found at this link: `https://github.com/bcatalin/esp8266-book/tree/master/Chapter7`.

The steps to start the server are:

1. Install Node.js and npm. Verify that both are present on your system:

```
catalin@plex:~/PROJECTS/websockserver$
catalin@plex:~/PROJECTS/websockserver$ node -v
v6.11.4
catalin@plex:~/PROJECTS/websockserver$ npm --version
3.10.10
catalin@plex:~/PROJECTS/websockserver$
catalin@plex:~/PROJECTS/websockserver$
```

2. Install a server's dependencies using the command `npm -v`:

```
catalin@plex:~/PROJECTS/websockserver$
catalin@plex:~/PROJECTS/websockserver$ npm install
npm WARN deprecated crypto@0.0.3: This package is no longer supported. It's now a built-in Node module.
you should switch to the one that's built-in.
[           ] \ fetchMetadata: sill mapToRegistry uri https://registry.npmjs.org/utils-merge
```

3. Edit the file `websocketserver/public/services/wsDataService.js` with your IP address of the server and the port used:

```
//wsDataService
angular.module('wsApp').factory('socket', function ($rootScope) {
    var socket = io.connect('//192.168.1.24:1234');

    return {
        on: function (eventName, callback) {
            socket.on(eventName, function () {
                var args = arguments;
                $rootScope.$apply(function () {
                    callback.apply(socket, args);
                });
            });
        },
```

4. Start the server with the command `node server.js` issued in the
   `websocketserver` directory:

```
catalin@plex:~/PROJECTS/websockserver$ node server.js
The magic happens on port 1234
Connected  socket id:HgmjiF_fAE3XE_3AAAAA
SOCK: connection - new WEB connection!!!!!
SOCK: RX connection => Send acc_ram with data
=====================================================
|ID| Web Socket ID                                  |
=====================================================
| 0| HgmjiF_fAE3XE_3AAAAA                            |
=====================================================

=====================================================
|ID| ACC ID      | Socket ID                        |
=====================================================
Connected  socket id:7-xIcezugppEdDXgAAAB
SOCK: connection - new ACC connection
{ acc_id: 'ACC_D357A3' }
=====================================================
|ID| ACC ID      | Socket ID                        |
=====================================================
| 0| ACC_D357A3 | 7-xIcezugppEdDXgAAAB |
=====================================================
{ acc_id: 'ACC_D357A3' }
=====================================================
```

In the preceding screenshot, you can see two connections: one from the web with the Web
Socket ID `HgmjiF_fAE3XE_3AAAAA` and another one from the ESP8266 module with the
`socket id: 7- xIcezugppEdDXgAAAB`.

Open a browser and point it to your server's IP address and port and you will see the
acceleration on a nice graph provided by `smoothieJS`:

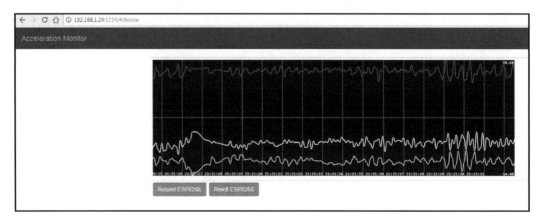

Pressing **Reboot ESP8266** will remotely reboot your module, and if you press the **Reinit ESP8266** button from the web page, the ESP8266 will reset all the data for Wi-Fi credentials, IP address, and port number.

You can add multiple modules on the same server, for each new connection, the server will add a new graphic and new buttons for it. In this way, you can monitor multiple sensors in the same page without refreshing it, or taking any action. This is very good if you want to provide a nice dashboard for your home automation platform.

As an improvement, you can add a time-series database such as InfluxDB (https://www.influxdata.com/) to store the received value, with your own desired persistence. To create a more elaborate dashboard, you can use Grafana (https://grafana.com/):

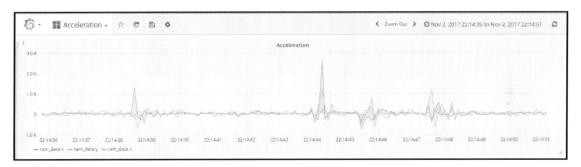

The server code consists of two parts:

1. Backend code that is responsible for receiving the connections from ESP8266 modules and web pages.
2. Frontend code that connects to the server and shows the nice graphs.

Backend code

The entire backend code is written in JavaScript and it is in the server.js file.

To create the server, the module provided by socket.io is used because socket.io provides real-time bi-directional event-based communication:

```
var server = http.createServer(app);
var io = require('socket.io').listen(server);
```

To receive messages, it is necessary to add a handler for them. In the `'connection'` event, when a message is received it means that a new ESP8266 acceleration module wants to connect to the server. Values for the ID and socket are retrieved from the `'data'` and added to the local list of previously connected ESP8266 acceleration modules:

```
socket.on('connection', function (data)
  {
    var acc_ram = new Object();
    acc_ram.socket_id = socket.id;
    var data_json = ParseJson(JSON.stringify(data));
    acc_ram.acc_id = data_json.acc_id;
    acc_ram.socket = socket;
    addACCObject(acc_ram);
    printACC();
    for(var webBrowsers = 0; webBrowsers < webConnections.length;
webBrowsers++)
    {
      var sessionID = webConnections[webBrowsers].socket;
      sessionID.emit('acc_ram', { acc_ram: data })
    }
  });
```

To inform all the connected browsers that a new ACC is ready to send data, the backend server code sends an `acc_ram` message to them and forwards the `data` object that contains the module ID.

On receipt of the message, the browser will construct dynamically graphical elements (canvas for drawing, buttons) for the new module.

When the JSON message type that contains values for the measured acceleration is received by the backend, the message is forwarded to all the browsers, and the values will become input data for the `smoothie.js` graphics:

```
socket.on('JSON', function (data)
  {
  for(var webBrowsers = 0; webBrowsers < webConnections.length;
webBrowsers++)
  {
   //send data to all connected browsers
   var sessionID = webConnections[webBrowsers].socket;
     sessionID.emit('acc_data', { acc_data: data });
  }
  });
```

For the messages received from the web page that are addressed to a specific ESP8266 module, we need to identify first the destination module based on the socket ID and send that message to the right module. Otherwise a reset command will be sent to all ESP8266 modules and I am sure that this is not what you intended to do:

```
socket.on('resetModule' , function (data)
  {
    for(var j=0; j< accConnections.length; j++)
    {
    var acc_m = accConnections[j];
       if(acc_m.acc_id == data.acc_id)
    {
     var s = acc_m.socket; //Get the socket
      s.emit("resetModule", {message: data} );
      return; //======>
    }
   }
  });
```

Public web page

The web page served by your Node.js server is a simple SPA developed with the BoostrapJS and AngularJS. The web page will try to connect to the server with a WebSocket connection, and after that it will send its own registration message, so the server can add its socket into its database.

The entry point for the acceleration values from ESP8266 but forwarded by the backend server is:

```
socket.on('acc_data', function(data)
  {
   for(var i=0; i < $scope.myacc_collection.length; i++)
   {
     if(data.acc_data.device_name == $scope.myacc_collection[i].acc_id)
     {
       $scope.myacc_collection[i].x = Number(data.acc_data.x);
       $scope.myacc_collection[i].y = Number(data.acc_data.y);
       $scope.myacc_collection[i].z = Number(data.acc_data.z);
       var currentDate = new Date().getTime();
       $scope.myacc_collection[i].axeX.append(currentDate,
Number(data.acc_data.x));
       $scope.myacc_collection[i].axeY.append(currentDate,
Number(data.acc_data.y));
       $scope.myacc_collection[i].axeZ.append(currentDate,
Number(data.acc_data.z));
        return;
```

```
      }
    }
  });
```

This function is receiving the actual data from the server and adding the values for the *X*, *Y*, and *Z* acceleration to the `smoothie.js`, using the `append` function.

Summary

In this chapter, we completed another important functionality that can be accomplished with ESP8266, real-time communication. You have learned how to stream real-time acceleration from an ADXL345 3 axes accelerometer to a backend Node.js server that will forward the received data to connected browsers. Data is drawn nicely in real time with `smoothie.js`. As a continuation of this chapter, I encourage you to store the received data in a time-series database, use Grafana as a display tool for your values, and why not send them over MQTT to an MQTT broker. Adding the database and a nice tool for displaying the values can turn this solution into a commercial one. You can develop a platform for storing and showing real-time data for other companies or private users.

8 Adding a Mobile Application to Your Smart Home

In previous chapters we discussed Blynk as a digital dashboard for your project. If you want to build your own mobile application that connects to your MQTT cloud you will find in this chapter an application starter code that allows you to have a basic mobile application in just a few minutes. Current mobile application code allows you to log in to `http://iotcentral.eu` and control your registered devices.

In this chapter we will address the following topics:

- Installing Docker
- Getting a development image for the Single Page application
- Getting the demo code for the mobile application
- Getting the application smart socket code for ESP8266
- Installing an existing firmware for an ESP8266 MQTT broker
- Producing the APK for Android devices

Installing Docker and using containers

A container image is a lightweight, standalone, executable package of a piece of software that includes everything needed to run it: code, runtime, system tools, system libraries, and settings. In this way you don't need to install lots of libraries and software, you can use an existing image and start a container from it.

We will use a container with Ionic and Android SDK that will allow you to develop and test a mobile application. At the end, you will have an APK file that needs to be signed using Google Play Console and after that you can roll it out to millions of people.

In the same Ubuntu 16.04 in the Virtual Box used before, we will install and configure Docker:

1. Install the GPG key in your system:

```
curl -fsSL https://download.docker.com/linux/ubuntu/gpg | sudo apt-key
add -
```

2. Add a Docker repository to APT sources:

```
sudo add-apt-repository "deb [arch=amd64]
https://download.docker.com/linux/ubuntu
$(lsb_release -cs) stable"
```

3. Update the package database with the new added repository:

```
sudo apt-get update
```

4. Install Docker Community Edition from the Docker repository instead of the Ubuntu repository:

```
apt-cache policy docker-ce
```

The output indicates that there are several versions available:

```
docker-ce:
  Installed: (none)
  Candidate: 17.09.0~ce-0~ubuntu
  Version table:
     17.09.0~ce-0~ubuntu 500
        500 https://download.docker.com/linux/ubuntu xenial/stable
        amd64 Packages
     17.06.2~ce-0~ubuntu 500
        500 https://download.docker.com/linux/ubuntu xenial/stable
        amd64 Packages
     17.06.1~ce-0~ubuntu 500
        500 https://download.docker.com/linux/ubuntu xenial/stable
        amd64 Packages
     17.06.0~ce-0~ubuntu 500
        500 https://download.docker.com/linux/ubuntu xenial/stable
        amd64 Packages
     17.03.2~ce-0~ubuntu-xenial 500
        500 https://download.docker.com/linux/ubuntu xenial/stable
        amd64 Packages
```

```
17.03.1~ce-0~ubuntu-xenial 500
    500 https://download.docker.com/linux/ubuntu xenial/stable
    amd64 Packages
17.03.0~ce-0~ubuntu-xenial 500
    500 https://download.docker.com/linux/ubuntu xenial/stable
    amd64 Packages
```

5. Now install Docker:

```
sudo apt-get install -y docker-ce
```

6. Verify your installed Docker version:

```
sudo docker version
Client:
 Version:      17.09.0-ce
 API version:  1.32
 Go version:   go1.8.3
 Git commit:   afdb6d4
 Built:        Tue Sep 26 22:42:18 2017
 OS/Arch:      linux/amd64
Server:
 Version:      17.09.0-ce
 API version:  1.32 (minimum version 1.12)
 Go version:   go1.8.3
 Git commit:   afdb6d4
 Built:        Tue Sep 26 22:40:56 2017
 OS/Arch:      linux/amd64
 Experimental: false
```

7. Start Docker daemon on every boot:

```
sudo systemctl status docker
docker.service - Docker Application Container Engine
   Loaded: loaded (/lib/systemd/system/docker.service; enabled; vendor
preset: enabled)
   Active: active (running) since Mon 2017-10-23 20:41:43 CEST; 46min
ago
     Docs: https://docs.docker.com
 Main PID: 12117 (dockerd)
   CGroup: /system.slice/docker.service
           ├─12117 /usr/bin/dockerd -H fd://
           └─12141 docker-containerd -l
unix:///var/run/docker/libcontainerd/docker-containerd.sock --metrics-
interval=0 --start-timeout 2m --state-dir /var/run/docker/libcontainerd
```

8. In order to run `docker` commands without the `sudo` in front of them we need to add our user in the Docker group:

```
sudo usermod -aG docker ${USER}
```

9. Now you need to log out and re-login to be able to run `docker` commands without `sudo`. Instead of that you can run this command:

```
su - ${USER}
```

10. Verify that your user is in the Docker group with:

```
id
```

The Docker group should be in the command output:

```
uid=1000(catalin) gid=1000(catalin)
groups=1000(catalin),4(adm),20(dialout),
24(cdrom),26(tape),27(sudo),29(audio),30(dip),44(video),46(plugdev),
109(netdev),119(scanner),120(lpadmin),121(sambashare),998(docker)
```

Now Docker is installed and configured to run every time the virtual machine is started. To complete our setup for the mobile application we need to get the image that will be used to build and develop the mobile app and some starting code for the mobile application.

Getting the development image

To get the development image from the Docker repository issue the command:

```
sudo docker pull agileek/ionic-framework
```

This will take some time, so be patient, but the time consumed to install all dependencies and all the required packages, compared to correcting errors is greater than this download.

At the end the image will be in the local repository. You can see what images are in your current repository by running the command as shown here:

```
catalin@plex:~$
catalin@plex:~$
catalin@plex:~$ docker images
REPOSITORY                TAG        IMAGE ID         CREATED          SIZE
agileek/ionic-framework   latest     559594ff121f     11 hours ago     4.5GB
catalin@plex:~$
catalin@plex:~$
```

Docker images

From the development image you can start how many containers you want. In each container, you can develop one application totally separate to another. The code for the application resides externally to the container, but it is accessible by the container to compile it and run it inside the container. The result of this phase will be an application that will run in your browser. At the end you can create a `*.apk` file and test it on your mobile phone:

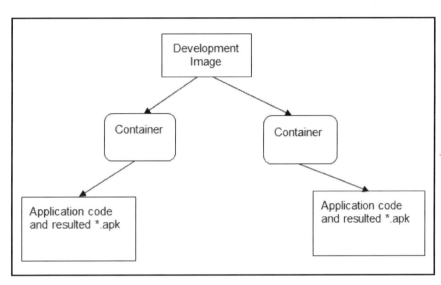

Now that we have the infrastructure built, let's get some code from GitHub and start a container with it:

```
mkdir ~/PROJECTS
cd ~/PREOJECTS
git clone https://github.com/bcatalin/Homy4
```

Now, in the directory `Homy4` there is some code that allows a user to enter its credentials for an `http://iotcentral.eu` account. After authentication, the application will get the connection details assigned for this account and will connect to the `iotcentral.eu` over WebSockets.

Start the container using the existing code. Basically, the directory where the code resides is internally mapped to the container by using the volume mapping:

```
docker run -it -p 8100:8100 -p 35729:35729 --name espbook -v
/home/catalin/PROJECTS/Homy4/:/myApp:rw agileek/ionic-framework
```

The switches that are used in the command are:

- `run`: This instructs Docker to start a new container.
- `-p 8100: 8100`: The container internal port `8100` is mapped externally to port `8100`. It will be accessed later by the browser. If you want to run multiple containers, change the external port to a different one. In this case the command will become `-p 8101:8100`.
- `-p 35729:35729`: This port is used for live reloads. If you modify the code (externally to the container) the application that runs inside the container will automatically reload itself. Again, if you need to run multiple instances of containers from the same image, don't forget to change the port.
- `--name`: You can give the container a name with numbers such as `5961e5e90592`. It is better to give an explicit name so that later you can remember what it was used for.
- `/home/catalin/PROJECTS/Homy4/`: This path, on the host machine, is where the downloaded code from Git exists.
- `/myApp`: This is the directory from the container where the code will be seen by the application in the container.
- `rw`: The mounting between the host system and the container is read and write.
- `agileek/ionic-framework`: This is the name of the image from your local repository.

After the creation of the container you can see its state with this command:

```
docker ps
```

To view all the containers which have started and stopped, you can use the following command:

```
docker ps -a
```

Now that the container has been started, open a browser in the host and navigate to `http://localhost:8100`. You should see a web page loaded into the browser inviting you to introduce a username and a password:

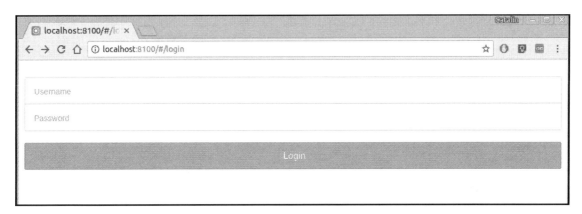

Now the size of the application is formatted for the browser, but since you are developing a mobile application it would be nice to see exactly how it looks on a mobile phone. For this you need to enter it in the **Developer Tools** mode. There are many modes to do that:

- Right-click with your mouse on the browser and choose **Inspect**
- Use the keyboard combination *Ctrl + Shift + I*
- From the menu choose **More Tools** and then select **Developer Tools**

After you are in **Developer Tools** you can go and change the look of the page using the *Ctrl + Shift + M* combination or you can click the image that looks like a phone and a tablet in the left corner.

Now the layout should be like this:

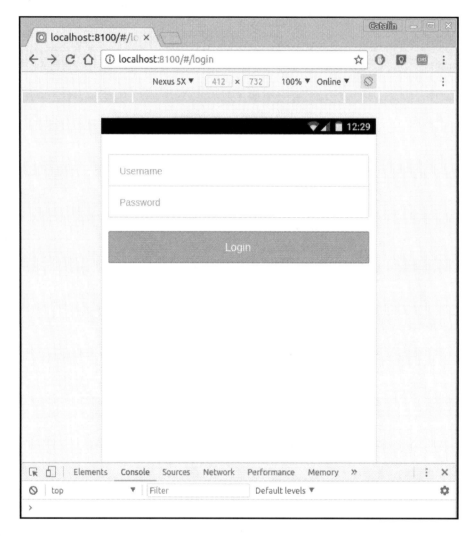

From the top bar you can select to see how it looks on a Nexus 5X, Nexus P, or iPhone, or you can change orientation of the screen and many other options.

Setting up the local broker

Now that the setup is in place, let's discuss what we want to achieve in this chapter. Later in this chapter, we will come back to the mobile application:

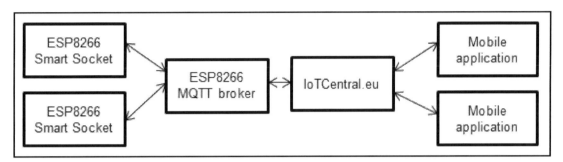

You have enough knowledge now to complete the entire system from ESP8266 code to your local broker and to the mobile application. To complete this chain we can start with the ESP8266. Let's create a simple plug code and let's use the PaaS service offered by `iotcentral.eu` as an authorization and cloud MQTT service:

1. Create an account and validate your email address on `iotcentral.eu`:

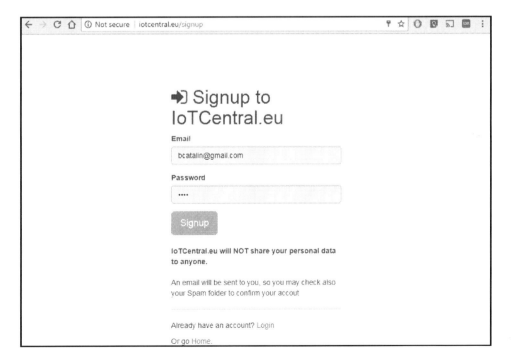

2. Get the `bondar.bin` binary image of a local MQTT broker and write it to a nodeMcu 4Mb board. Power off and then on the board:

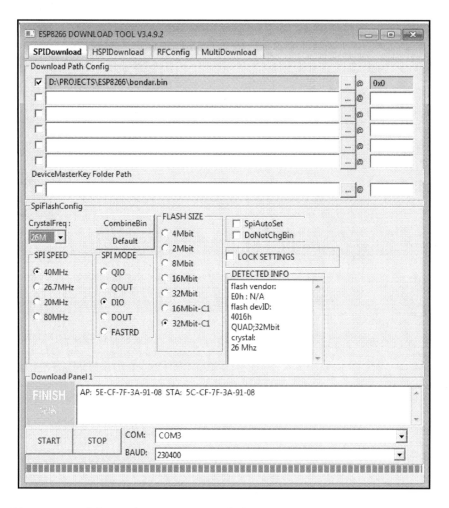

3. Use your mobile application to search for an Access Point named `Bondar_XXXXXXX` where `XXXXXX` are the latest six digits from the MAC address.

4. Connect to it and use the password `12345678` if it is requested. Navigate with your phone browser to address `192.168.4.1` and in the web page enter the same credentials that you have used for the `iotcentral.eu` account. The local broker will connect to the `iotcentral.eu` platform and will register itself.

On your devices page on `iotcentral.eu` you should be able to see your newly registered local broker. Using the local broker on an ESP8266 is not mandatory, but it simplifies your code on ESP. If you choose not to use a local broker, you need to connect directly to the cloud MQTT broker on `iotcentral.eu`. In this case we need to get your allocated topic and add more logic in your code to handle this:

On `https://github/bcatalin/demoapp` is the code that we will use as the ESP8266 code. Get the code and write it to the ESP8266.

After the ESP8266 is rebooted, go to your phone and search for on Access Point named **ESPap**. Connect to it and navigate with your browser to the address `http://192.168.4.1` like you did for the local EP8266 MQTT broker. In the page presented by the ESP8266, fill the Wi-Fi credentials, the username, and password used for `iotcetral.eu`, the Amazon Alexa name you want to call your module to turn something ON or OFF, and your time zone (this is not implemented, you can just do it as an exercise):

ESP8266 code specifications

The requests for the ESP8266 code and you need to subscribe to topics:

```
/<TOPIC>/plug/command or <TOPIC>/plug/command
```

In this case you connect the ESP directly to `iotcentral.eu`.

The required message to be received by the ESP8266 in order to trigger its GPIO 12 is:

```
{"device_name":"ESP_3A9108", "type":"plug", "state":1}
```

Here:

- `Device_name`: Is the device's name that we want to trigger.
- `Type`: Is the type of device. In this case it is `plug`.
- `State`: Is the desired state of the GPIO 12. In this case, we want to change the state to *ON*.

```
/<TOPIC> /status/update or <TOPIC>/status/update
```

In this case, there is direct connection to `iotcentral.eu` without a local broker. Receiving any message on this topic will trigger ESP8266 to send its status and its device status messages. The mobile application is sending the message:

```
{"1":"1"}
```

On this topic, when it starts, in order to get a status and state from all your devices. You will need to publish messages on the se topics:

```
/<TOPIC>/plug/status or <TOPIC>/plug/status
```

The content of the message published needs to have this format:

```
{"device_name":"ESP_3A9108", "type":"plug", "state":1}
```

Here:

- `Device_name`: Is the name created by the application based on a MAC address.
- `Type`: Is the device type. In this case, it is a plug.
- `State`: Is the current state of the GPIO 12 pin. In this case, 1 means ON.

`/<TOPIC>/device/status or <TOPIC>/device/status` without local broker.

The message that is published on this topic is describing the status for this device (IP address, SDK version, uptime, and more):

```
{"device_name":"ESP_3A9108","type":"plug","ipaddress":"192.168.8.222","alex
a":"Coffee
maker","bgn":3,"sdk":"1.5.3(aec24ac9)","version":"1039","uptime":"0 days
00:40:12"}
```

Based on the received messages the mobile application is constructing its interface and displays devices, grouping them by type:

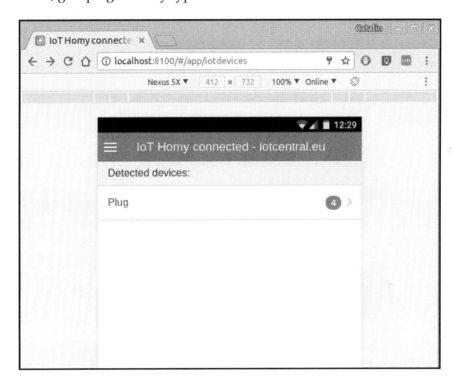

A mobile application is connected to `iotcentral.eu` and has discovered four devices having the same types of **Plug**. Clicking on the **Plug** types will show all the devices found for this type.

If you see a message in the console saying that the access has been blocked because of the cross-origin header, install a Chrome plugin that allows you to have cross-origin calls. For this find the extension named *Allow-Control-Allow-Origin*. The cross-origin problems will not exist on your mobile phone:

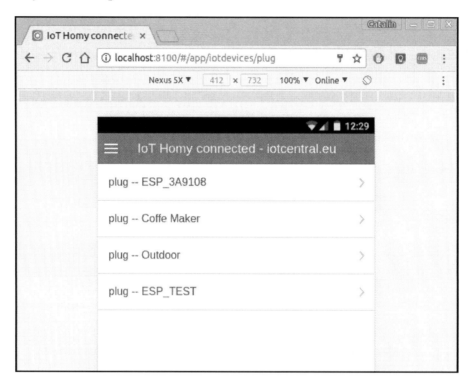

In the extended list for all devices that have the type `plug`, there is also our device `Coffee Maker`. Here at the beginning, the name of the device is shown as `ESP_` followed by the last six digits from the MAC address, but you can give it a friendly name by swapping the desired plug to the left and seeing the **Edit alias** button:

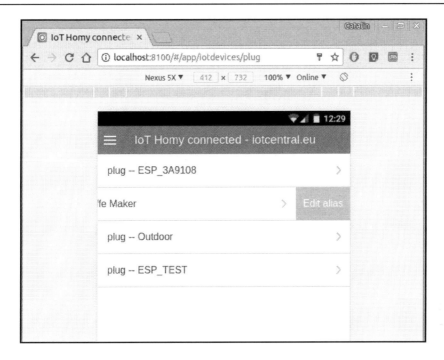

You can change the encoded name to a friendlier name:

Clicking **Save** will save the new alias name in the local storage of the application and will be shown every time this device is seen by the application.

If you are selecting from all devices, with the same type being **Coffee Maker**, the mobile application will show the action page from where you can trigger the ON or OFF plug (in fact the GPIO 12):

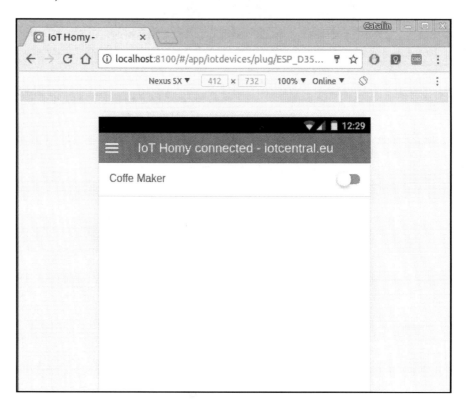

In the lower part of the screen you will see two tabs, one is for the device status and the other is for device details:

You can see the content of the message published on the topic `<TOPIC>/device/status`, the connected IP address of the ESP8266, its up time, software version, SDK version with which it was compiled, and the friendly name assigned during the initial setup.

After you change the mobile application to add new devices, or to look and feel differently, you need to create the `.apk` application that needs to be installed to your phone.

In order to do this, first you need to log in to the container with the following command:

```
docker exec -it espbook bash
```

This command will log in to a container named `espbook` and will start the bash shell.

Navigate to `/myApp/www` and issue the command that will produce the APK:

```
ionic cordova build android
```

After 30 seconds you will have your APK, ready for you to test it on a real phone at the location: `/myApp /platforms/android/build/outputs/apk`

The `apk` file needs to be signed in order to be used. There are a lot of tutorials on the internet on how to do it and how to publish your mobile application on Google Play.

This demo mobile application is now on Google Play. Search for `Homy4` and install it. Don't forget to create an account on `iotcentral.eu` first and to use the `demoapp` on an ESP8266.

Summary

In this chapter, you have learned how to use Docker to create a development environment for creating and using a mobile application. On the ESP8266 side you have learned the topics and messages that the module needs to have in order to be able to integrate into a system composed from a cloud MQTT and a mobile application. The code for ESP8266 in the demo app is too big to be presented here, but it covers all the ESP8266 chapters of the book: how to connect to Wi-Fi, how to store data in SPIFFS, how to connect to an MQTT broke, and how to subscribe and publish messages on topics. It can be a good start for a Smart Plug device since it is a fully functional example.

On the mobile part, code that exists in the GitHub example is fully operational with the `iotcentral.eu` platform and with the demo app. Looking to the code a learning more on how to develop and mobile application with Ionic and Cordova, you will be able to easily add new devices such as temperature monitoring, controlling air conditioner units, and controlling intra red equipment.

You now have all the knowledge to change your house to a smart house. Using the ESP8266 as the fog computing, you can now create a multitenant MQTT cloud and even a smart mobile application. with all this knowledge you can even start to build your own product and sell it on the market since you don't depend on any other platform and everything is in your own domain of knowledge.

Index

Made in the USA
Lexington, KY
29 November 2018